Multicultural Programs
for Tweens and Teens

Edited by Linda B. Alexander and Nahyun Kwon
for the Young Adult Library Services Association

American Library Association
Chicago   2010

Dr. Linda B. Alexander, a YALSA member, teaches graduate students in the School of Library and Information Science at the University of South Florida. Her main interests and courses include children's literature, materials for young adults, and multicultural materials for children and young adults. She is also active in her state's library associations. She has published articles about GLBTQ (gay, lesbian, bisexual, transgender, questioning) issues and the use of differing Cinderella versions for addressing diversity, and library instruction. She maintains a website for multicultural Cinderella versions at www.cas.usf.edu/~lalexand/Cinderella.htm, and another one for multicultural materials for children and young adults at www.cas.usf.edu/~lalexand/multicultural.htm.

Dr. Nahyun Kwon teaches at the Department of Library and Information Sciences of Myungji University in Seoul, Korea. Previously, she taught in the Department of Library and Information Sciences at the University of South Florida. Her specialties are information services to diverse groups, information-seeking behaviors, service evaluation, and information literacy. She has a repertoire of published articles in these areas. Listings of her interests and research can be found at www.mju.ac.kr/nkwon/menu/home/index.jsp.

The paper used in this publication meets the minimum requirements of American National Standard for Information Sciences—Permanence of Paper for Printed Library Materials, ANSI Z39.48-1992. ⊗

Library of Congress Cataloging-in-Publication Data

Multicultural programs for tweens and teens / edited by Linda B. Alexander and Nahyun Kwon for the Young Adult Library Services Association.
    p. cm.
  Includes bibliographical references and index.
  ISBN 978-0-8389-3582-8 (alk. paper)
  1. Children's libraries—Activity programs—United States. 2. Young adults' libraries—Activity programs—United States. 3. Multicultural education—Activity programs—United States. 4. Ethnology—United States—Juvenile literature—Bibliography. 5. Ethnology—Juvenile literature—Bibliography. I. Alexander, Linda B. II. Kwon, Nahyun. III. Young Adult Library Services Association.
  Z718.3.M85 2010
  027.62'5—dc22

        2009050679

ISBN-13: 978-0-8389-3582-8

Printed in the United States of America
14 13 12 11 10   5 4 3 2 1

Contents

Acknowledgments

Our sincere gratitude goes to Saritza Legault and Ana Lopez, our graduate assistants of the School of Library and Information Science at the University of South Florida, who worked so diligently on compiling and formatting the materials. Thanks are also extended to the students who have taken our multicultural materials course and developed creative and authentic programs of the various cultures in our country.

Introduction

The face of our nation is continually shifting.

We live in a society that is perpetually becoming more culturally diverse. As librarians and information specialists, it is imperative that we provide materials for furthering knowledge about various cultures that coexist in our society; furthermore, it is essential that we who disseminate information promote diversity for future generations. Healthy youth development involves the provision of a scholastic environment that supports and advances the social, emotional, spiritual, physical, moral, and cognitive development of our youth.[1] As librarians and educators, we are in a position to effectively provide such an environment. Therefore, we need to rise to the occasion and welcome multicultural awareness by becoming more familiar with the multifaceted character of our society. We should respect other cultures and motivate interest in their unique mores and behaviors. *Multicultural Programs for Tweens and Teens* is a survey that can help librarians and media specialists pave the way to greater awareness and interest in the differing cultures, by introducing students to each culture's background, religion, beliefs, ethics, manners, cuisine, and traditions.

Although this book presents an introduction to the inclusion of multi-culturalism, it should be noted that student exposure to diversity must be ongoing. School curriculum and public library youth services should begin to consider how they will integrate multicultural education as a long-term project and goal. Research has shown that most schools do indeed set aside special days for cultural events, but not many have ongoing programs promoting multicultural awareness.[2] *Multicultural Programs for Tweens and Teens* is geared to help readers begin the integration process; rather than simply using this source for one event, it is our hope that people use it multiple times for all the cultures inclusively, and continue to incorporate more and more diversity education.

Teaching Multiculturalism through Literature

Schwallie-Giddis, et al., point out that linguistically and culturally diverse students are continually challenged by problems derived from racial, ethnic, linguistic, and religious discrimination, as well as stereotyping; these dilemmas, in the end, lead to the students disengaging from their schools, and sometimes result in drop outs.[3] Thus, teaching about multicultural diversity via literature will be effective for minority youth to develop positive identities of their own, as they live and thrive in this melting pot called America.

Multicultural material is not just for minority children and young adults. Wham, Barnhart, and Cook questioned whether reading multicultural material to white children would affect their beliefs about different cultures.[4] Their results suggest that, without exposure to multicultural material, children's feelings regarding other cultures can become more negative and perhaps more fixed. That finding is frightening. In a society where our culture is becoming more multifaceted, it is imperative that "mainstream" educators and librarians, as well as our youth, be armed with multicultural-mindedness. In short, having access to multicultural materials and programs will guide youth of all backgrounds, and, in the end, help them become more aware and accepting of other cultures.

As librarians and educators, we understand the importance and role of books in teaching youth about different cultures. There are countless teens and tweens whose lives have been enriched by reading the works of Laurence Yep, Ashley Bryan, and Julia Alvarez, to name only a few. So the programs presented in *Multicultural Programs for Tweens and Teens* not only offer awareness through the programs themselves and all of the activities involved, but also give young participants an introduction to the literature. This way, the

learning process need not end when the program is over. Students can simply pick up a book and continue to learn.

Designed for Tweens and Teens of All Backgrounds

Multicultural Programs for Tweens and Teens covers various cultural groups with
several programs devoted to each group. Each program surveys a specific
culture as well as guidelines and ideas formatted for public libraries and
school media centers. These programs are designed with youth from those
specific cultures in mind, so that they may learn a little bit more about themselves or even bask in the joy of getting the chance to share their heritage with
others. For those who would be experiencing the culture for the first time, or
have some slight knowledge already, these inclusion programs are built to
introduce the culture and also give youth (and sometimes their families) an
opportunity to partake in multicultural awareness. Being introduced to new
cultures may even spark interest in their own culture. Youth may begin to
see how different cultures sometimes do things differently and wonder how
it applies to their own.

Additionally, and perhaps most significantly, it is important to instill diversity in the minds of our youth. Being—or not being—from a specific culture
may sometimes be a source of discomfort for youth trying to assert themselves and make their way through school and life; these events give educators and librarians the chance to familiarize students with aspects that may
seem alien.

Community Integration: Get Them into Libraries

The public library and school media center's role must be multifaceted in
order to meet the needs of the multicultural community. By introducing
multicultural materials to youth, we may begin to motivate them to take
an interest in their local library or media center. Through these inclusion
programs, teachers, librarians, and media specialists will be given the chance
to display a part of their collection, in turn sparking interest. Additionally,
by housing the inclusion programs in the library or media center, students
will be given the opportunity to better familiarize themselves with the center. Because to many, the library may seem an intimidating place, this is an
opportunity to reinforce the image of the library as a community center
and an important resource for information. Therefore in the case of public
libraries, these events should be open to the general public, giving potential patrons the opportunity to experience their neighborhood libraries.

Moreover, by holding such events as these, libraries and media centers will be allowed the chance to present themselves as community centers and outreach providers, where gaining knowledge can be enjoyable.

However, it does not just take a larger multicultural collection or more multicultural children's programs. Rather it requires the cooperation of teachers, librarians, and parents to make multiculturalism an integral part of the school's curriculum and the public library's services. Programs may be just the beginning in terms of expanding teens' and tweens' perceptions of other cultures, but they are a good start. Public libraries and school media centers can also work with local organizations to help broaden the library's patron base and bring multiculturalism to the forefront.

Our Youth Can Become Lifelong Library Users

Because many of these inclusion programs involve browsing library materials as well as interaction with electronic sources via library computers, youth can begin to better understand the nature of the library's more traditional functions. By learning how to use the library, youth can then naturally continue to be library users into adulthood. Starting with young patrons, who as they grow up may begin to integrate the idea of library use for information-seeking and pleasure reading into their lives, will simultaneously help them feel a part of their society. As adults, they can continue to use libraries for information-seeking and pleasure reading, as well as for community socialization. The promotion of information literacy will aid and empower youth; they will eventually be better able to find, evaluate, and use information not only for school projects and their future academic goals, but also within all aspects of their lives.[5]

How to Use This Book

In the spirit of scholarship and multicultural community, *Multicultural Programs for Tweens and Teens* is a compilation of library and information science graduate student inclusion and awareness project assignments. The contributors have developed the programs based upon the objectives and requirements of a graduate course in "Multicultural Materials for Young Adults and Children" for prospective librarians and school media specialists, developed by one of the authors. Borrowed from the cultures introduced within the course, the inclusion and awareness programs in this book are the finished product of students' own particular interest in a particular culture studied.

Included in each program is a list of easy-to-reference points that will enable users to either simply find some ideas or fully create an event. Each program is then divided by specific headings providing details about the event created. "Age Level" and "Duration of Library Program" are the first two headings, allowing users to quickly browse through the source in search of what is most applicable to their group and time frame. Subsequently, "Introduction and Background" to the program gives educators, librarians, and media specialists the opportunity to familiarize themselves with the history and culture of the tradition or event. A brief section on "Overall Goal" is also provided to help program leaders understand the motivation behind the inclusion program; this way, with a goal in mind, the readers may then taper or add to the program while still working toward the same ideologies. "Relevance to the Community Served" is followed by details of the "Activities" and "Preparation," a more in-depth description of what the program entails: what type of activities the event will comprise, how to prepare for such an event, and what the procedures are in the planning and execution of the program. "Cost and Materials" informs of an approximate cost estimated to prepare the program. In addition to the local Friends of the Library group and the library "kitty," a list of resources the library or media center may draw on is often provided to lend a helping hand.

Although each program includes an approximate cost, these estimates simply give professionals an idea of what the maximum cost could be. However, many libraries and media centers will be able to conduct these events at very little or no cost at all. Through the local institutions themselves, parent financial contributions and active participation, and local community foundations, these programs can be easily planned. Below are just a few examples of foundations existing to help with expenses:

> **Bring Me A Book Foundation, www.bringmeabook.org.**
> Bring Me A Book (BMAB), an award-winning literacy 501(c)(3) nonprofit, is committed to ensuring that all children are exposed to high-quality children's literature during the first years of their lives. BMAB provides libraries with quality hardcover children's books and read-aloud training to more than 400,000 children, parents, and teachers at more than 1,010 sites.
>
> **Council on Foundations, www.cof.org.**
> The Council on Foundations' mission is to provide

the opportunity, leadership, and tools needed by philanthropic organizations to expand, enhance, and sustain their ability to advance the common good. The council's members include more than two thousand grant-making foundations and giving programs worldwide.

First Book, http://register.firstbook.org.
First Book is a nonprofit organization with a single mission: to give children from low-income families the opportunity to read and own their first new books. They provide an ongoing supply of new books to children participating in community-based mentoring, tutoring, and family literacy programs.

Association for Library Trustees, Advocates, Friends and Foundations, www.ala.org/altaff.
The Association for Library Trustees, Advocates, Friends and Foundations (ALTAFF, formerly ALTA and Friends of Libraries USA) provides resources, services, and networking opportunities for Friends, trustees, and foundations across the country to increase and enhance their efforts on behalf of libraries of all types.

Each program includes a bibliography of the materials consulted. These bibliographies not only function to help librarians, media specialists, and educators with the collection development of their event, but can be used as a simple reference tool: some may have students already interested in a specific culture, so in that event, all one needs to do is flip to the specific chapter and browse through the titles. Finally, "Additional Materials" may include ready-to-customize language for fliers, handouts, and other materials necessary to the program.

Now, are you ready to begin your exciting journey of exploring various aspects of other fascinating cultures?

Notes

1. Patrick Jones, "Connecting Young Adults and Libraries in the 21st Century," *Australasian Public Libraries and Information Services* 20, no. 2 (2007): 48–54

2. Pat Schwallie-Giddis, Kristina Anstrom, Patricio Sánchez, Victoria Sardi, and Laura Granato, "Counseling the Linguistically and Culturally Diverse Student: Meeting School Counselors' Professional Development Needs," *Professional School Counseling* 8, no. 1 (2004): 15–23.

3. Ibid.

4. Mary A. Wham, June Barnhart, and Greg Cook, "Enhancing Multicultural Awareness through the Storybook Reading Experience," *Journal of Research and Development in Education* 30, no. 1 (1996): 1–9.

5. Jones, "Connecting Young Adults and Libraries."

CHAPTER 1

Exploring African American Culture

Famous African American Women Everyone Should Know

By Lisa Kothe

Age Level
12–14 years

Duration of Library Program
Several sessions of 45–60 minutes each

Introduction and Background
While men like Martin Luther King Jr. and Frederick Douglass were great contributors to American society and played important roles in our history, there are hundreds of lesser-known African American women who should be familiar choices for students to research.

This program will introduce young adults to selected famous African American women, and make them aware of other African American women they may want to research and get to know further.

Overall Goal
The overall objective of this program is to introduce students to African American women with whom they may not be familiar and for participants to

understand the important contributions of these women to their fields and the growth of this country.

A secondary objective is to familiarize students with library resources. Students (grouped into teams) will use library databases, encyclopedias, and books to complete a matching game, included in "Activities" below.

Relevance to the Community Served

This presentation introduces children to lesser-known female African Americans. It could also be adapted for Women's History Month. This age group studies history as part of the curriculum, and students need to see themselves in historical role models.

Activities

1. Introductions (self and each other)
2. Present the program's overall goal and reason for taking the time to talk about famous African American women.
3. Play the matching game (15 minutes). Group students into teams. Teams can use materials provided in presentation (see bibliography) and library databases (biography site or other online resources). Matching game handouts will be distributed and teams have fifteen minutes to complete the answers using library databases. While the game is being played, listen to a Marian Anderson CD in background.
4. Review the matching game (8 minutes). Winners get chocolate or another snack. Then present all participants with the same candy.
5. Hear selected readings (30 minutes). Ask for volunteers to read aloud for three to five minutes each. Use this list of important African American women in history:

   - Ask for a volunteer to read the author's note at the end of *Wilma Unlimited,* by Kathleen Krull. Briefly discuss the career of Wilma Rudolph, an American athlete who overcame poverty and illness.
   - Ask for a volunteer to read the section on Shirley Chisholm from *Let It Shine,* by Andrea Pinkney. Briefly discuss the career of Shirley Chisholm, the first African American woman elected to the U.S. Congress and a serious candidate for president of the United States.

- Ask for a volunteer to read from Pam Ryan's *When Marian Sang,* from page 22 to 27. Share the accompanying pictures. Briefly discuss the career of Marian Anderson, a singer who faced racism and was denied bookings in certain places because of her skin color.
- Ask for a volunteer to read from *Powerful Words*, by Wade Hudson, pages 138 to 139. Briefly discuss the career of Stephanie Tubbs Jones, a congresswoman from Ohio.
- Ask for volunteer to read from *Powerful Words,* pages 154 to 155. Briefly discuss the career of Toni Morrison, the first African American woman to win the Nobel Prize for Literature.
- Ask for a volunteer to read from *Women of Hope,* by Joyce Hansen, page 29. Share pictures and briefly discus the career of Mae Jemison, the first African American woman to travel into space.
- Ask for a volunteer to read from *Women of Hope,* page 19. Share the picture and briefly discuss the career of Maya Angelou, an accomplished African American poet and memoirist. Listen to Angelou read "On the Pulse of Morning," the poem she read at President Bill Clinton's inauguration. (See bibliography for CD information.) Pass around *The Complete Collected Poems of Maya Angelou.*

6. Add a link to the Reading Chain (5 minutes). Students will write the name of a book written by their favorite African American author, or a biography or autobiography of a famous black American male *or* female, on a strip of paper. Connect the papers by taping strips together in a chain, which can be used in a display for Black History Month to provide library users with reading suggestions.
7. Wrap up. Thank everyone for coming. Ask for completion of the program evaluation.

Preparation

The public librarian should contact school media specialists in the local area one month prior to the program to determine if reports for Black History Month are a requirement for their students. The public librarian can then better prepare the program to assist students in their research needs.

Cost and Materials

Approximate cost: $50–$100

- CD player/speakers
- Books and music CD (see bibliography)
- Matching game (multiple copies)
- Materials to make a Reading Chain—paper and markers
- Snacks for "winners" of the matching game and all participants

Bibliography

Anderson, Marian, and Pam Muñoz Ryan. Illus. by Brian Selznick. *When Marian Sang: Selected Songs from Marian Anderson's Repertoire*. With CD-ROM. New York: Scholastic; with BMG Special Products.

Selected songs from Marion Anderson's repertoire, including "Deep River" and "He's Got the Whole World in His Hands."

Angelou, Maya. *The Complete Collected Poems of Maya Angelou*. New York: Random House, 1994.

A compilation of the works of Maya Angelou, including her inauguration poem, "On the Pulse of Morning."

Angelou, Maya. *The Maya Angelou Poetry Collection*. Audiocassette. New York: Random House Audio, 1999.

A collection of poems read by Maya Angelou. Includes "Just Give Me a Cool Drink of Water," "I Shall Not Be Moved," "Oh Pray My Wings Are Gonna Fit Me Well," and "On the Pulse of Morning."

Bridges, Ruby. *Through My Eyes*. New York: Scholastic Press, 1999.

A heart-wrenching autobiography that includes provocative articles, interviews, and photographs.

Hansen, Joyce. *Women of Hope: African Americans Who Made a Difference*. New York: Scholastic Press, 1998.

A compilation of twelve short biographies about courageous African American women whose persistence and vision gave society hope and inspiration, plus a list of additional notable African American women who made a difference.

Harper, Judith E. *Maya Angelou*. Journey to Freedom series. Chanhassen, MN: Child's World, 1999.

A biography about Maya Angelou. Contains numerous photographs and quotes from Ms. Angelou.

Hart, Philip S. *Up in the Air: The Story of Bessie Coleman*. Minneapolis, MN: Carolrhoda Books, 1996.

A biography of Bessie Coleman, who became the first African American female pilot.

Hudson, Wade. *Powerful Words: More Than 200 Years of Extraordinary Writing by African Americans.* New York: Scholastic, 2004.

> Collection of over thirty inspiring essays, speeches, and words of wisdom by African Americans who shaped the American community from colonial to contemporary times. Contains author's notes and chronology.

Krull, Kathleen. Illus. by David Diaz. *Wilma Unlimited: How Wilma Rudolph Became the World's Fastest Woman.* San Diego: Harcourt, 1996.

> Picture book biography of Wilma Rudolph, the first African American women to win three gold metals in a single Olympics. A good read-aloud for children through sixth grade.

Pinkney, Andrea Davis. Illus. by Stephen Alcorn. *Let It Shine: Stories of Black Women Freedom Fighters.* San Diego: Harcourt, 2000.

> Ten stories about African American women who faced inequality, prejudice, and numerous obstacles, and who helped our country triumph in the battle for civil rights.

Plowden, Martha Ward. Illus. by Ronald Jones. *Famous Firsts of Black Women.* Gretna, LA: Pelican Publishing, 1993.

> A look into the lives of twenty African American women who opened the doors for others to follow.

Ryan, Pam Muñoz. Illus. by Brian Selznick. *When Marian Sang: The True Recital of Marian Anderson; The Voice of a Century.* New York: Scholastic Press, 2002.

> An award-winning picture book that tells the story of Marian Anderson and how her perseverance and courage made her one of the country's finest singers.

Sullivan, Otha Richard. *African American Women Scientists and Inventors.* Black Stars series. New York: Wiley, 2002.

> This book explores known and unknown African American scientists and inventors who made advances in medicine, engineering, and technology.

Winegarten, Ruthe, and Sharon Kahn. *Brave Black Women: From Slavery to the Space Shuttle.* Austin: University of Texas Press, 1997.

> This book profiles the history of black women from all walks of life, from slavery to the present day.

Webliography

About.com. "Notable African American Women." http://womenshistory .about.com/library/bio/blbio_list_afram.htm.

> Resources about famous African American women from early American slavery to the twenty-first century, including the Harlem Renaissance and the civil rights movement.

Additional Materials

THE MATCHING GAME

1. Phillis Wheatley _____

2. Toni Morrison _____

3. Rosa Parks _____

4. Wilma Rudolph _____

5. Bessie Coleman _____

6. Coretta Scott King _____

7. Maya Angelou _____

8. Belinda Womack _____

9. Marian Anderson _____

10. Shirley Chisholm _____

11. Patricia Roberts Harris _____

12. Mary McLeod Bethune _____

13. Jackie Joyner-Kersee _____

A. An accomplished singer and the first American soloist to sing with the New York Metropolitan Opera. She is remembered for her Easter Day performance in front of the Lincoln Memorial.

B. Olympic gold medalist in the heptathlon. She is considered to be one of the best female athletes of all time. Postretirement, she works with disadvantaged children.

C. Founder of the National Council of Negro Women, director of Negro Affairs of the National Youth Administration, and special adviser on minority affairs to President Franklin D. Roosevelt.

D. Author and winner of the Nobel Prize in Literature in 1993.

E. Considered to be the first African American poet. This former slave published a collection of poems in 1773.

F. Local Tampa Bay blues/jazz singer who gives back to her community.

G. First African American woman to serve as a U.S. ambassador and in a cabinet position.

H. First African American woman to be elected to the U.S. Congress.

I. Often known as the mother of the modern-day civil rights movement, due to her role in the Montgomery, Alabama, bus boycott.

J. First American woman to win three gold medals in a single Olympic games (1960).

K. Continued the work of her husband as a civil rights activist.

L. First African American woman to obtain pilot's license and become a pilot.

M. This PhD poet and best-selling author recited her original work at President Clinton's first inauguration.

Key: 1—E; 2—D; 3—I; 4—J; 5—L; 6—K; 7—M; 8—F; 9—A; 10—H; 11—G; 12—C; 13—B

Celebrating the Harlem Renaissance

By Amy G. Peterson

Age Level

11–15 years

Duration of Library Program

60–70 minutes

Introduction and Background

Planned as the culmination of the monthlong celebration and study of African American history in February, this program is designed for an evening presentation at a school media center. At the program, students will present reports to educate attendees about the Harlem Renaissance, accompanied by music, food, poetry, and visual art from that era.

Elements of this program can be redesigned to fit any age group or library setting. With older students in a media center, the research and presentations can be more complex, and focus with greater depth on the societal and historical aspects that brought about the Harlem Renaissance. If being planned for a public library, community and library groups, speakers, and interested patrons can be substituted for student presenters and performers.

Overall Goal

Attendees and participants will learn about the history, people, and artistic output of the Harlem Renaissance and understand the impact of its art and culture on our modern era.

Relevance to the Community Served

Influential beyond measure, the artists of the Harlem Renaissance had a huge impact on artistic, social, popular, and entertainment cultures. Although students learn the broad strokes of African American history in school, cultural elements are often glossed over in favor of studying important historical occurrences and accomplishments. The focus of this program is to expose young people, their families, and the community to important figures and works of the Harlem Renaissance.

Activities

This program consists of informational presentations and demonstrative performances, accompanied by visual art slideshows, music, and food.

As conceived for a school media center, student presentations will be based on assigned topics relating to the Harlem Renaissance at the beginning of African American History Month, which they will be researching at the media center with staff assistance. Working cooperatively with language arts, social studies, and history curriculum, students will write brief presentations based on lessons and discussions about the historical context of the Harlem Renaissance in their classrooms. This curricular exploration would be supported through schoolwide displays and morning announcement segments.

In a nonschool setting, local African American community groups for young people may be a good place to start when searching for speakers. Participants in teen and tween library programs and clubs are also a readily available resource.

It is suggested that the performance aspects of this program be planned to use local resources. A school or community poetry or spoken word group could perform at the program. If the school or community has a jazz band, they could perform in lieu of recorded music. Dramatic groups found either at school or in the community might be interested in performing excerpts from the many plays written during the Harlem Renaissance. A dance troupe at the school or in the community might be interested in performing some of the dances from the Harlem Renaissance era.

The program will start with presenters providing a general introduction to the Harlem Renaissance, including societal and historical factors that contributed to, and defined, the era known as the Harlem Renaissance. Following the introduction, presentations will highlight important figures in the literature of the Harlem Renaissance. This discussion of literature would serve as an introduction to performances planned on a local level, whether they are students reading poems and excerpts, or full-blown performances by local groups.

The next presentations will discuss musicians and dance steps popularized during the Harlem Renaissance. These presentations can lead into music and/or dance performances. In lieu of live performance groups, clips of music performances from the DVD *Harlem Renaissance: The Music and Rhythms That Started a Cultural Revolution* can be played.

Then presentations will focus on the visual artists of the Harlem Renaissance, followed by presentations about the fashion and slang of the era, and a final summary, including a brief promotion of highlighted materials in the local collection, and thanks to all contributors, performers, presenters, and collaborators. At this point, food will be served. Traditional food found in many of the restaurants in Harlem during the Harlem Renaissance will be served buffet-style. While attendees are eating, a slideshow highlighting artists and fashion of the era can be shown, accompanied by recorded music or live music performances. Local exhibitions can be planned in lieu of or in tandem with a slideshow.

To help program planners visualize the subjects that will be covered in the program, an annotated outline is included below.

Preparation

Student participants will be doing a significant amount of research and writing prior to the program. The media specialist must ensure that students have access to research materials, and the research know-how to locate the information they need. To weave together a cross-curricular approach, the staff must hold collaborative planning sessions. Staff conducting the program will ready exhibition materials, arrange for any groups that are interested in participating in the program, prepare the program venue with furniture arrangement and decorations, and promote the event. Local collection materials need to be pulled and selected for promotion and display during the program. Arrangements for food and serving must be made ahead of time.

Cost and Materials

The costs associated with this program would be for food, performers, and promotion. It is recommended that any performers who would charge are asked to waive their fee, and that promotion is done in-house, as part of an assumed yearly promotion budget. Money for food and other items can be funded by local library monies (such as annual book sales, Friends associations, etc.), donations, and grants. Any element of the program can be redesigned for a zero budget cost, such as omitting the food portion of the event.

Bibliography

Against the Odds: The Artists of the Harlem Renaissance. DVD. PBS Home Video, 1993.

> Using archival footage, this documentary explores the personalities of the visual artists who helped shape the Harlem Renaissance.

Angelou, Maya. Illus. by Jean-Michel Basquiat. *Life Doesn't Frighten Me.* Edited by Sara Jane Boyers. New York: Stewart, Tabori, and Chang, 1993.

> Maya Angelou's poem illustrated by Jean-Michel Basquiat. Addresses issues of courage, fear, and fearlessness. Includes biographies of both author and artist.

Bolden, Tonya. Illus. by Ansel Pitcairn. *Portraits of African-American Heroes.* New York: Dutton Children's Books, 2003.

> Artist Ansel Pitcairn illustrates twenty biographical essays by Tonya Bolden. The essays and portraits cover a range of outstanding African Americans, from dancer Judith Jamison to Supreme Court justice Thurgood Marshall.

Cannarella, Deborah. *Zora Neale Hurston: African American Writer.* Chanhassen, MN: Child's World, 2003.

> A brief biography of the great African American writer, whose love of stories as a child led to her successful career as a writer of plays, poems, short stories, and novels.

Cooper, Floyd. *Coming Home: From the Life of Langston Hughes.* New York: Philomel Books, 1994.

> This book serves as an introduction to poet Langston Hughes. Hughes is one of the most prominent and notable American poets of the twentieth century.

Duggleby, John. *Story Painter: The Life of Jacob Lawrence.* San Francisco: Chronicle Books, 1998.

> Twenty-five collected paintings highlight this biography of Jacob Lawrence. Lawrence grew up during the Harlem Renaissance and uses his brush to tell stories of human struggles and triumphs.

Ehrlich, Scott, and Nathan Irvin Huggins. *Paul Robeson.* New York: Chelsea House, 1988.

> Singer, actor, athlete, and social activist Paul Robeson was one of the most accomplished, successful, and controversial men of his day. In addition to covering his accomplishments, this biography compares some of Robeson's ideas about equality and civil rights with the ideas of some of his contemporaries, like Marcus Garvey and W. E. B. du Bois.

Giovanni, Nikki. *Shimmy Shimmy Shimmy Like My Sister Kate: Looking at the Harlem Renaissance through Poems.* New York: Henry Holt and Company, 1996.

> Giovanni brings together a tremendous collection of poetry that she ties together with her own commentary. This work provides some background and an introduction to the Harlem Renaissance. Includes poems from Langston Hughes, Gwendolyn Brooks, and Countee Cullen.

Hardy, P. Stephen, and Sheila Jackson Hardy. *Extraordinary People of the Harlem Renaissance.* Extraordinary People series. New York: Children's Press, 2000.

> The Harlem Renaissance was one of the most important creative periods in U.S. history. This work provides information on the musicians, poets, composers, writers, choreographers, and photographers who helped create and maintain this cultural milestone.

Harlem Renaissance: The Black Poets. DVD. Carousel Film and Video (New York) and WCAU-TV (Philadelphia), 1971.

> Readings and visual interpretations of poems out of the Harlem Renaissance. Includes a reading of an essay by W. E. B. du Bois.

Haskins, James. *The Harlem Renaissance.* Brookfield, CT: Millbrook Press, 1996.

> Covers the milestones achieved by the artists and intellectuals of black America during the 1920s and 1930s in Harlem, New York.

Hill, Laban Carrick. *Harlem Stomp! A Cultural History of the Harlem Renaissance.* New York: Little, Brown, 2003.

> A history book that explains why African Americans from across the nation were drawn to Harlem in the years leading up the Harlem Renaissance. Richly illustrated, this work serves as a serious introduction to a key moment in American history.

Hughes, Langston. Illus. by Romare Bearden. *The Block: Poems.* New York: Viking, 1995.

This collection of thirteen poems by Langston Hughes celebrates the New York City neighborhood of Harlem. Hughes's celebratory poetry is illustrated by the collage painting of Romare Bearden.

Lewis, Zoë. Illus. by Dan Burr. *Keisha Discovers Harlem.* Portland, ME: Magic Attic Press, 1998.

While trying to find a subject for her school assignment, Keisha learns about the music and writing of the Harlem Renaissance.

Manera, Alexandria. *Bessie Smith.* Chicago: Raintree, 2003.

The biography of one of the most famous blues singers of all time. Bessie Smith was widely popular during the 1920s and is still considered one of the greatest blues singers today.

Medina, Tony. Illus. by R. Gregory Christie. *Love to Langston.* New York: Lee and Low, 2002.

These fourteen poems tell the story of Langston Hughes. Explanatory notes at the back of the book help explain some of the history Hughes witnessed.

Michelson, Richard. Illus. by Earl B. Lewis. *Happy Feet: The Savoy Ballroom Lindy Hoppers and Me.* Orlando, FL: Harcourt/Gulliver Books, 2005.

A young boy feels a close association with the Savoy Ballroom because it opened the same night he was born. The Savoy is legendary and the boy hopes one day to have his dancing debut there.

Monroe, Judy. *Duke Ellington: Jazz Composer.* Mankato, MN: Capstone Press, 2005.

This biography of Duke Ellington describes the tremendous influence he had on American music.

Muse, Daphne, selector. Illus. by Charlotte Riley-Webb. *The Entrance Place of Wonders: Poems of the Harlem Renaissance.* New York: Harry N. Abrams, 2006.

A collection of poems from the artists who helped shape the Harlem Renaissance. Includes brief biographies of the poets, and represents well-known artists as well as newly discovered writers.

Raatma, Lucia. *The Harlem Renaissance: A Celebration of Creativity.* Chanhassen, MN: Child's World, 2003.

An introduction to the Harlem Renaissance for young readers. This tremendous outpouring of creativity is one of the most important artistic and cultural moments in U.S. history.

Schoeneberger, Megan. *Ella Fitzgerald: First Lady of Jazz.* Fact Finders series. Mankato, MN: Capstone Press, 2005.

Introduction to jazz singing great Ella Fitzgerald. Fitzgerald performed at Carnegie Hall twenty-six times and recorded more than two hundred albums.

Swingin' Uptown Renaissance in Harlem. DVD. Kultur, 2004.

> Music was an integral part of the Harlem Renaissance. This documentary looks at the history and impact of that music by speaking with the performers and historians of the era.

Weik, Mary Hays. Illus. by Ann Grifalconi. *The Jazz Man.* New York: Atheneum, 1966.

> The story of a young boy with a lame leg. His life changes when a jazz man moves in across the court.

Webliography

Artcyclopedia. "The Harlem Renaissance." www.artcyclopedia.com/history/harlem-renaissance.html.

> Information about the Harlem Renaissance, including a chronological listing of artists.

Oliver, Lynn. "The food timeline." www.foodtimeline.org/index.html.

> Time line of food from water and salt to modern times. Includes many links.

Soulfood Online. http://soulfoodonline.net.

> Recipes and resources related to soul food.

West, Sandra. "We are a dancing people." www.nathanielturner.com/weareadancingpeople.htm.

> Information and history about African American dancing styles.

Additional Materials

The Harlem Renaissance Outline

Note: This outline is not meant to be comprehensive, but rather is a guide to subject assignments for student research or topics for other types of presenters to highlight.

I. **Societal and Historical Factors Contributing to the Rise of the Harlem Renaissance**
    A. African American Migration to the North
    B. World War I

II. **The Beginning of the Harlem Renaissance**
    Due to the deployment of American troops, many jobs were left vacant. Many African Americans migrated to northern industrial cities in search of employment.
    A. Harlem Settlement
    B. Important Figures and Factors
    C. Dates

III. Important Figures Contributing to the Harlem Renaissance

Around the turn of the twentieth century, there were many African American people working for equality that in many ways, either directly or indirectly, helped the Harlem Renaissance to come about.

    A. W. E. B. Dubois, founder of *The Crisis* magazine, was a crucial element to the progress of the Harlem Renaissance

    B. James Weldon Johnson, founder of the NAACP and writer

    C. Mary McLeod Bethune, educator, civil rights leader, and advisor to Langston Hughes

    D. Charles S. Johnson, writer and anthropologist

    E. Marcus Garvey, writer and activist

    F. Charles S. Johnson, sociologist and writer

    G. Booker T. Washington, educator, activist, and community leader

    H. Ruth Standish Baldwin and George Edmund Haynes, founders of the National Urban League

IV. Sponsors of the Harlem Renaissance

The Harlem Renaissance was made possible by many sponsors of mixed heritage and motivation. An element of this subject to highlight is the difficult situation that a sponsored artist faced, further complicated by the prejudices held by many white sponsors.

    A. A'Lelia Walker, heiress of Madam C. J. Walker's beauty product empire

    B. Charlotte Osgood Mason, philanthropist

    C. Harmon Foundation. Founded by real estate developer William Harmon, it gave substantial monies to African American artists, especially notable for its contribution to the visual art exhibitions of African American artists

    D. Works Progress Administration (WPA; later years of the Harlem Renaissance)

    E Carl Van Vechten, writer and publisher

V. Defining the Cultural Influences and Artists of the Harlem Renaissance

The artistic output of this era encompassed many media and had a huge impact on popular and artistic culture.

    A. Music/Performers

        Many feel that the Harlem Renaissance was the beginning of

jazz becoming pop music that reached a racially mixed audience. Performers to highlight are listed below.

1. Duke Ellington
2. Cab Calloway
3. Count Basie
4. Fats Waller
5. Jelly Roll Morton
6. Louis Armstrong
7. Paul Robeson
8. Ella Fitzgerald
9. Billie Holiday
10. Bessie Smith
11. Marian Anderson
12. Josephine Baker

B. Dance

Many of the dances that people think of as defining the roaring twenties started in Harlem nightclubs. Each of these dances has a fascinating origin in African American culture; for instance, it is known that the Charleston is a version of an African dance called the Juba.

1. Jitterbug—encompassed many styles of jazz/swing dancing
2. The Charleston
3. The Lindy or the Lindy Hop
4. The Shag
5. The Black Bottom/The Mess Around
6. Trucking
7. The Big Apple
8. The Shimmy

C. Literature

The first time that many African American voices were heard, some of the most amazing and moving works of our time came from this era in literature that encompassed poetry, fiction, drama, and nonfiction.

1. Langston Hughes
2. Countee Cullen
3. Claude McKay
4. Jean Toomer
5. Zora Neale Hurston

      6.   Richard Wright

      7.   James Weldon Johnson

      8.   Wallace Thurman

      9.   Nella Larson

      10. Arna Botemps

D. Visual Arts

Encompassing a vast array of media, the visual artists of the Harlem Renaissance broke new ground by painting expressions of their heritage and exploring the works of the European masters.

      1.   Aaron Douglas

      2.   Lois Mailou Jones

      3.   Palmer Hayden

      4.   William H. Johnson

      5.   Jacob Lawrence

      6.   Sargent Claude Johnson

E. Fashion and Slang

The popular trends in mainstream fashion and slang of this historical period were influenced greatly by the people and artists of Harlem.

VI. The End of the Harlem Renaissance

Celebrating African American Artists and Illustrators

By Ann M. Maloney

Age Level

All age groups (and can incorporate evening sessions to include families)

Duration of Library Program

45-minute lecture plus 15-minute question-and-answer period

Introduction and Background

The work of African American artists and illustrators has not received the exposure that white artists and illustrators have enjoyed in the United States. This is slowly being corrected as more publishers and museums promote works by African Americans. The development of awards, such as the Coretta Scott King Award, has helped to publicize the body of work created by this group. Several prominent art historians have written excellent books about African American art. One of those books is featured in this program: *The Other Side of Color* by David C. Driskell.

The public library can play a significant role in the promotion, and exposure to the public, of this often overlooked group. For example: the library has art books, art instruction books, how-to art videos, biographies of artists, and art magazines. In addition, many public libraries have art galleries. A conscious effort to include African American artists in collection development could result in wider exposure for those artists. Community programs and art exhibits featuring African American artwork can also help raise public awareness. Links to websites that feature collections including multicultural art can also be promoted.

Overall Goals

- To raise awareness of the work of African American artists and illustrators
- To present the public library to the community as a multicultural center

Relevance to the Community Served

Communities include many different ethnic groups; this highlights one of those groups. This program strives to educate all groups in the community since many may not be aware of the contributions made by various historical figures.

Activities

The program can cover only a small selection of art due to time constraints. In the interest of time, we are focusing on the work of three African American artists and illustrators, namely Floyd Cooper, Faith Ringgold, and Bryan Collier. Each artist has a children's or young adult book that can be displayed. Other artists will be mentioned and some other art is on display but will be only briefly mentioned.

Use the bibliography to direct participants to many wonderful books and websites that will increase their knowledge of the world of African American artists and illustrators.

Narratives

David C. Driskell is an art historian. He is also the private art curator for Bill and Camille Cosby as well as other collectors. In the book's introduction, Bill Cosby writes,

Not until after my tour of duty in the Navy . . . did I realize why the museum world had not stimulated within me
a desire to own art. When I visited these places of high culture, I saw little evidence that people of color could become
visual artists or were worthy of being shown as positive subjects on canvas. I do not recall seeing any images of black
people as subjects in sculpture yet stereotypical images
abounded. I began to ask myself whether the absence of
black images, except stereotypic ones, was deliberate in our
mainstream museums. When would I see the art of African Americans displayed beside English, German, Irish,
French, and Italian artists?

This is a worthy question to examine. African American artists have been
creating art all through American history. Portrait artists such as Joshua
Johnston were commissioned (sometimes by whites) as early as 1799. Robert S. Duncanson, landscape artist, painted in the 1800s. Augusta Savage (a
woman) did sculpture of intense beauty in the 1900s. The Harlem Renaissance produced many talented artists in all forms: painting, sculpture, photography, and illustration. There was an African American comic strip artist named Jackie Ormes; the University of Michigan Press has published a
book about her work. Gordon Parks was a famous photographer whose work
is highly acclaimed.

Let us turn to the artist and illustrators we are featuring today. The first
artist selected is Faith Ringgold. The book we will review is *Tar Beach,* written and illustrated by Ringgold. She won a Coretta Scott King Award for the
illustration of the book in 1992, and it was selected as a Caldecott Honor
Book. The author is also well known for her story quilts. She has a master
of arts degree from City College of New York and worked for almost twenty
years as a public school teacher. Ringgold was a leader in the equal rights
movement and cofounded Women Students and Artists for African American Liberation (WSABL) in the 1960s. Through her protest work, and pro-
tests with others, the Whitney Museum of American Art in New York City
featured two African American woman artists in its 1971 Contemporary
Black American Artists in America exhibition. Ringgold's work is very urban
and contemporary. She has written several children's books and an autobiography. Ms. Ringgold's work is currently in museum collections as diverse
as the Spencer Museum of Art at the University of Kansas and the Guggen-
heim Museum of Art in New York City (Driskell 2001, pp. 195–196).

Floyd Cooper is a talented artist and author who has won Coretta Scott King Honors in 1994, 1995, and 1999. He has written over fifty children's books and illustrated more than two thousand book covers. He has commercial accounts as diverse as Budweiser, Hallmark, and Avon. He has also won an NAACP Image Award. *Tough Boy Sonatas* by Curtis L. Crisler is an example of Cooper's illustration work. This is a book of poetry—strong, gritty poetry. Crisler writes in the voices of young men living and dying in the streets of Gary, Indiana. Cooper chooses to illustrate by showing the faces, bodies, and expressions of these boys almost exclusively in black and white. He uses a subtractive process where he completes the painting then uses an eraser to draw. Other works by Cooper feature soft, flowing colors with delicate detail beautifully illustrating picture books for the younger child. Cooper does school visits featuring his work. Perhaps some of you will want to contact him about visiting your schools. His is an example of a highly successful career in art encompassing many types of work (www.floydcooper.com).

The third artist featured today is also a Coretta Scott King Honors and Award winner many times over. Bryan Collier grew up on the eastern shore of Maryland and currently lives in Harlem, New York. He works largely in collage and watercolor. Today we are viewing his illustration of *Rosa* by Nikki Giovanni. The work is realistic, historically time appropriate, and colorful. The book includes a four-page fold-out illustration. Collier is a featured artist on the Reading Is Fundamental website (www.rif.org/art/illustrators/collier.mspx) and has a website of his own (www.bryancollier.com) featuring his work. He, like Cooper, does school presentations. On his website, he states, "In my art and in my life I'm looking for the thread that connects all of us and I'm looking for that seed of individuality."

There are so many wonderful, talented artists and illustrators to learn about and view. Today we just touched on a few. Please continue to seek information about them, discuss them, and lobby your local libraries and museums to showcase their work.

Preparation

Bookmarks, posters in the library, invitations sent to middle and high school art departments, banner on local public access TV channel, and mention in monthly library newsletter.

The program planner may create a handout from the narrative information about the three artists for the participants to take home with them.

Cost and Materials

Approximate cost: $0–$100

Costs can be offset by local sponsors, such as Friends of the Library, or a local printer might contribute printing in return for their name on the printed materials.

- A copy of each work cited
- Printing of invitations, bookmarks, and posters
- Postage

Bibliography

Parr, Ann. Photographs by Gordon Parks. Illus. by Kathryn Breidenthal. *Gordon Parks: No Excuses.* Gretna, LA: Pelican Publishing, 2006.

> This biography presents to young readers the life of Gordon Parks, who overcame difficulties growing up in segregated Kansas and later became one of the most outstanding African American photographers in America. The title came from his mother, who used to tell Parks, "What a white boy can do, you can too—and no excuses." The illustrations are interspersed in the book to demonstrate a scene from the text.

Colen, Kimberly, and Wendell George Brown. *Faith Ringgold.* Audiocassette. New York: Scholastic, 1993.

> An interview with artist and author Faith Ringgold, whose book *Tar Beach* received a 1992 Caldecott Honor and a Coretta Scott King Illustrator Award. She recounts her childhood in Harlem in the 1930s and 1940s, her love for books, and how she became a best-selling author of children's books.

Crisler, Curtis L. Illus. by Floyd Cooper. *Tough Boy Sonatas.* Honesdale, PA: Wordsong, 2007.

> This collection of poems reflects Crisler's experiences growing up in Gary, Indiana, a town beset with poverty and crime.

Drew, Bernard Alger. *100 More Popular Young Adult Authors: Biographical Sketches and Bibliographies.* Santa Barbara, CA: Libraries Unlimited, 2002.

> Biographies and works are illustrated in this collection of one hundred popular young adult authors.

Driskell, David C., Camille O. Cosby, Bill Cosby, and René Hanks. *The Other Side of Color: African American Art in the Collection of Camille O. and William H. Cosby, Jr.* San Francisco: Pomegranate, 2001.

> Nearly one hundred works of art from the collection of Camille and Bill Cosby provide a wide-ranging and in-depth look at African American art.

This collection spans work created over the last two centuries. David Driskell provides background and explains the significance of the work.

Duggleby, John. *Story Painter: The Life of Jacob Lawrence.* San Francisco: Chronicle Books, 1998.

Twenty-five collected paintings highlight this biography of Jacob Lawrence. Lawrence grew up during the Harlem Renaissance and uses his brush to tell stories of human struggles and triumphs.

Emmerling, Leonhard. *Jean-Michel Basquiat: 1960–1988.* Köln, Germany: Taschen Deutschland, 2003.

Jean-Michel Basquiat, who started as an enigmatic street graffiti artist in New York in the late 1970s, later received fame as a successful neo-expressionist artist in the 1980s, and died of a drug overdose at the age of 27 in 1988.

Farrington, Lisa E. *Art on Fire: The Politics of Race and Sex in the Paintings of Faith Ringgold.* New York: Millennium Fine Arts Publishing, 1999.

Examines Faith Ringgold's use of political and human themes in her work, including her distinguished painted story quilts.

Farrington, Lisa E. *Faith Ringgold.* San Francisco: Pomegranate, 2004.

Ringgold is an innovative American artist known for her wide range of art, including printmaking, sculptures, and paintings. She is often identified with her painted story quilts, which deal with themes of human dignity and African American empowerment.

Giovanni, Nikki. Illus. by Bryan Collier. *Rosa.* New York: Henry Holt and Company, 2005.

Tells the story of Rosa Parks, whose refusal to give up her seat on a Montgomery, Alabama, city bus in 1955 became emblematic of the civil rights movement that was sweeping the United States. Parks became one of the most important figures in the movement and the events that followed.

Goldstein, Nancy. *Jackie Ormes: The First African American Woman Cartoonist.* Ann Arbor: University of Michigan Press, 2008.

This biography of a pioneering African American cartoonist includes a selection of her cartoons and comic strips that deal with social issues such as racial segregation, cold war, inequality, and the environment, among other pressing issues of the times.

Haskins, James. *The Harlem Renaissance.* Brookfield, CT: Millbrook Press, 1996.

Chronicles the milestones achieved by the artists and intellectuals of black America during the 1920s and 1930s in Harlem, New York.

Jillette, Penn, et al. *Behind the Scenes. Vol. 2 Theatre, Sculpture and Photography.* DVD. First-Run Features (New York), 2003.

This DVD presents life, works, and creative work processes of many renowned artists, including Carrie Mae Weems, the award-winning African American photographer.

Kirsh, Andrea, Susan Fisher Sterling, and Carrie Mae Weems. *Carrie Mae Weems*. Washington, DC: National Museum of Women in the Arts, 1993.
Photographer Carrie Mae Weems's work examines gender and class through the lens of her experience as an African American.

Monroe, Gary. *The Highwaymen: Florida's African American Landscape Painters.* Gainesville: University Press of Florida, 2001.
Young black artists in 1950s Florida painted images of a dreamlike paradise and sold them door-to-door and from the trunks of their cars. Includes sixty-three images of work by the highwaymen.

Parks, Gordon. *Eyes with Winged Thoughts.* New York: Atria Books, 2005.
A collection of photographs and poems by the extraordinary American artist, writer, musician, poet, journalist, and filmmaker Gordon Parks. Parks is notable for his great success in popular and artistic achievements.

Ringgold, Faith. *Tar Beach.* New York: Crown Publishers, 1991.
Using art from her story quilt from 1988, Ringgold has taken both the setting and the text and captured a child's dreams while reminding the reader of the social injustices of the adult world. The theme is both universal and contemporary.

Webliography

Bryan Collier's website. www.bryancollier.com.

Floyd Cooper's website. www.floydcooper.com.

Faith Ringgold's website. www.faithringgold.com.

Kids at Random House, Faith Ringgold. www.randomhouse.com/kids/catalog/author.pperl?authorid=25610.

Reading Is Fundamental, Bryan Collier. www.rif.org/art/illustrators/collier.mspx.

Celebrating African American History Month

By Benjamin Mittag

Age Level

12–18 years

Duration of Library Program

60–120 minutes per session, held in the afternoon or evening

Introduction and Background

This program is designed for a public library celebration of African American History Month. Conducted throughout the entire month of February, this program is designed to celebrate the cultural heritage of African Americans and their achievements in politics, literature, music, drama, art, cinema, entertainment, sports, science, and beyond.

Overall Goal

This program will provide a succession of events that celebrate the importance of African American cultural history and achievements, enriching the knowledge of those who attend and take part.

Relevance to the Community Served

This program will help African Americans in the community celebrate their collective cultural history, while exposing those not of African American heritage to the many achievements and struggles that have been overcome by this diverse group.

Activities

This celebration takes place during the entire month of February. Each week of the month will be designated for the following themes:

> Week 1: Sociopolitical Figures Who Made History, such as Thurgood Marshall, Booker T. Washington, Condoleezza Rice, and Barack Obama. Program participants will read books (see bibliography) on well-known historical figures, as well as write a paper on "Why I think this person was important to the history of our country." A Best Paper contest will honor the writer of the winning paper. Youth will have the week to research and write a paper. In preparation for this week, fliers will be created by library staff and distributed to the schools for posting on bulletin boards. Written research and essay-type papers would be due to the library reference desk by noon on Sunday at the end of Week 1 for judging by social science teachers. First-, second-, and third-place winners will be announced on the local radio station the following afternoon.
>
> Week 2: Achievements in Entertainment, Music, Arts, and Literature. Students will read books on the artists this week. Those planning the program will come up with written questions and answers about various artists, such as LL Cool J, Bob Marley, Queen Latifah, Will Smith, and Tyra Banks. Participants will be divided into two teams with a leader for each. The contest will follow the Battle of the Books style of finding which team knows more answers to the popular culture questions. The winning team will receive prizes. This activity can be duplicated daily over the course of the week and can take up to

sixty minutes, depending on the number of questions created. Fliers will be created announcing this contest on the upcoming Saturday. Participants will obtain bibliographies from the reference desk listing books from which contest questions will come. All participants will be at the library by two o'clock, ready to begin forming the teams. Depending on the number of participants, there may be two large teams or four to six teams that can play tournament games, and teams can be designated by using numbers drawn at the door upon arrival.

Week 3: African American Sports Stars and Scientific Achievements includes such well-known players as Michael Jordan, Jackie Robinson, and Arthur Ashe. Movie Night is scheduled for the third Saturday night of the month, and there are various sports-themed movies that can be selected from the library's DVD collection. The one suggested for this program is about basketball great Kobe Bryant. "Kobe Doin' Work: A Game in the Life" is an ESPN documentary presented by Spike Lee, a well-known African American movie director. The Teen Advisory Group (TAG) can sponsor this event by making the preparations, including seating, as well as popcorn and other refreshments. The Movie Night is free to all teens.

Week 4: Important African American Women includes Shirley Chisholm, Maya Angelou, Coretta Scott King, Michelle Obama, and others in history. A book discussion will be held on the final Saturday of Black History Month on books selected by the teens earlier that week. Each will read different biographical or autobiographical titles of important black women before the book discussion date. Participants will be asked to discuss various aspects of their lives, including the environment in which they grew up, struggles and challenges, common qualities driving their success in their fields, and influences on the larger American society. The invited speaker of the week or the librarian can be the moderator of the discussion. TAG members who participate will be responsible for the seating arrangement and refreshments.

These events will include presentations by notable speakers on African history and culture on such diverse topics as art, music, literature, sports, science, and politics. The events can also include African American spoken word poetry, photography exhibits, film showings, and musical performances such as traditional African drum circles.

Preparation

In preparation for this month-long celebration, the librarian will distribute information about the events through fliers, posters, book displays, and community advertisement (community public radio and television), as well as through the library's website and e-mails to patrons. The librarian will also secure volunteers for displays and set up of events, as well as selecting speakers and artists to orate and perform for the various events.

Cost and Materials

Approximate cost: minimal, with much of the materials donated or paid for by Friends of the Library.

- Promotional materials, such as printed and e-mailed handouts, and morning show announcements. Handouts will outline the activities for each week so that students can read and prepare in advance of the week's activities.
- Decorations and refreshments, if any. ALA-published READ posters of various celebrities can be used as decorations.
- Visual and audio equipment
- Prizes for winning teams

Bibliography

Sociopolitical Figures Who Made History

Beckner, Chrisanne. *100 African-Americans Who Shaped American History*. San Francisco: Bluewood Books, 1995.
    Concise biographies of a wide range of significant African Americans. Entries are arranged chronologically. This work makes for both a great reference tool and a wonderful history book.

Bell, Janet Cheatham, and Lucille Usher Freeman. *Stretch Your Wings: Famous Black Quotations for Teens.* Boston: Little, Brown, 1999.

Includes over four hundred quotations from African Americans with photographs and biographical notes.

Boyd, Herb. *We Shall Overcome.* Naperville, IL: Sourcebooks, 2004.

Recounts the history of the civil rights movement and its inherent struggles. Includes archival photographs and two audio CDs with narration from Ossie Davis and Ruby Dee.

Davis, William. *Barack Obama: The Politics of Hope.* Stockton, NJ: OTTN Publishing, 2008.

Written before the forty-fourth president won his historic election, this biography touches briefly on Obama's childhood, but focuses mainly on his adult, political life.

Halliburton, Warren J. *Historic Speeches of African Americans.* New York: Franklin Watts, 1993.

A compendium of speeches from African Americans covering the course of U.S. history. Each speech includes biographical information of the speech maker, and historical background to put the speech into context.

Harlan, Louis R. *Booker T. Washington: The Wizard of Tuskegee, 1901–1915.* New York: Oxford University Press, 1983.

This is part of a substantive two-volume biography. The first volume won the prestigious Bancroft Prize in 1973, awarded by historians for the best work of history in a given year. Not for young children, this weighty tome is suitable for late high school and early college young adults.

Hubbard-Brown, Janet. *Condoleezza Rice: Stateswoman.* New York: Chelsea House, 2008.

A biography of the first African American woman to serve as U.S. secretary of state. Secretary Rice's life has blazed a trail for other women. Her tenure as secretary of state is only the latest in a series of firsts that she has accomplished.

Katz, William Loren. *Black Pioneers: An Untold Story.* New York: Atheneum Books for Young Readers, 1999.

The oft-told tales of American expansion into the west during the nineteenth century frequently omits the stories of African American pioneers. William Loren Katz provides some of the stories of the men and women who moved west to find their freedom, while continuing the battle to end slavery.

Levine, Michael L. *African Americans and Civil Rights: From 1619 to the Present.* Phoenix, AZ: Oryx Press, 1996.

Historical overview of the African American experience in North America. Ten chapters cover the period from the first enslaved Africans to arrive on the shores of the British colonies to the struggles that continue after the twentieth-century civil rights movement. Includes some short biographies, a chronology, a glossary, and suggestions for further reading.

McLeese, Don. *Thurgood Marshall: Discover the Life of an American Legend.* Vero Beach, FL: Rourke Publishing, 2003.

Biography of the first African American to serve on the Supreme Court of the United States. Marshall is also notable for his role in the landmark Brown v. Board of Education case.

Rennert, Richard Scott. *African American Answer Book: Biography; 325 Questions Drawn from the Expertise of Harvard's Du Bois Institute.* New York: Chelsea House, 1995.

Brief biographies of notable African Americans.

Rummel, Jack. *African-American Social Leaders and Activists.* A to Z of African Americans series. New York: Facts on File, 2003.

Focusing on African American social reformers and political activists, this book looks at 164 different African Americans and their impact on history.

Schraff, Anne E. *Booker T. Washington: "Character Is Power."* Berkeley Heights, NJ: Enslow Publishers, 2006.

Examines the life of the trailblazing African American educator who became one of the most important and influential African American men of the late nineteenth century.

Schuman, Michael. *Barack Obama: "We Are One People."* Berkeley Heights, NJ: Enslow Publishers, 2008.

A solid introductory biography to the life of the forty-fourth president of the United States.

Thoennes Keller, Kristin. *Booker T. Washington: Innovative Educator.* Minneapolis, MN: Compass Point Books, 2007.

Biography of the man who established the Tuskegee Normal and Industrial Institute in Alabama. Over the course of his storied career, Washington never stopped fighting to increase educational opportunities for African Americans.

Thomas, Garen Eileen. *Yes We Can: A Biography of Barack Obama.* New York: Feiwel and Friends, 2008.

A more personal than political biography, this work relies heavily on aspirational and inspirational quotations by the forty-fourth president.

Wade, Linda R. *Condoleezza Rice.* Hockessin, DE: Mitchell Lane Publishers, 2005.

This profile of the first black female U.S. secretary of state ranges from her childhood in Alabama to her appointment as the first black female national security advisor and secretary of state.

Achievements in Entertainment, Music, Arts, and Literature

Baughan, Brian. *LL Cool J.* Hip-Hop series. Broomall, PA: Mason Crest, 2007.

Takes a look at the life of James Todd Smith, the actor and rapper better known as LL Cool J.

Berne, Emma Carlson. *Snoop Dogg.* Hip-Hop series. Broomall, PA: Mason Crest, 2007.

    Biography of popular entertainer and rap artist Calvin Broadus, better known to the world as Snoop Dogg.

Clinton, Catherine. Illus. by Stephen Alcorn. *I, Too, Sing America: Three Centuries of African-American Poetry.* Boston: Houghton Mifflin, 1998.

    This work collects examples from three centuries of African American poetry. Each poem is illustrated by Stephen Alcorn, and includes a brief biography of the poet.

Dance, Daryl Cumber. *From My People: 400 Years of African American Folklore.* New York: W. W. Norton, 2002.

    A collection of folktales and more. Includes tales on subjects as diverse as food, hairstyles, and more.

Dean, Tanya. *Della Reese.* Philadelphia: Chelsea House, 2002.

    A biography of the popular actress, singer, and minister. Those who only know Reese from her role on *Touched by an Angel* may be surprised at the many other accomplishments she has had in her life.

Dillon, Leo, and Diane Dillon. *Rap a Tap Tap: Here's Bojangles—Think of That!* New York: Blue Sky Press, 2002.

    Multiple Caldecott winners, the Dillons turn their talents to the story of Bill "Bojangles" Robinson. These graceful paintings wonderfully capture the grace and style of this important American dancer.

Dolan, Sean. *Bob Marley.* Philadelphia: Chelsea House, 1997.

    A biography of the influential Jamaican musician who popularized reggae music around the world until his untimely death from cancer.

Galens, Judy. *Queen Latifah.* Detroit: Lucent Books, 2007.

    A short biography of well-known rapper, model, and actress Dana Elaine Owens, better known as Queen Latifah.

Gisnash, Sahara. *Salt-n-Pepa.* Hip-Hop Biographies series. New York: Rosen Publishing Group, 2006.

    This book tells the story of this all-girl band from their formation to their break-up.

Gutner, Howard. *Up, Up, and Away! The Mae Jemison Story.* New York: McGraw-Hill School Division, 1999.

    Growing up in Chicago in the 1960s, Mae Jemison knew the only astronauts were men. However, she never doubted that one day she, too, would have her chance. In 1992 Jemison became the first African American woman to travel into space.

Haskins, James. *Black Theater in America.* New York: Crowell, 1982.

    This history of African American theater covers drama, comedy, and music from the antebellum period to the present. Includes bibliography and index.

Hill, Ann E. *Tyra Banks: From Supermodel to Role Model.* Minneapolis, MN: Lerner, 2009.

> Biographical in nature, this book discusses how Tyra's life has been changed by her celebrity from model to role model. For teen readers.

Hill, Laban Carrick. *Harlem Stomp! A Cultural History of the Harlem Renaissance.* New York: Little, Brown, 2003.

> A history book that explains why African Americans from across the nation were drawn to Harlem in the years leading up the Harlem Renaissance. Richly illustrated, this work serves as a serious introduction to a key moment in American history.

Hooper, James. *Nelly.* Hip-Hop series. Broomall, PA: Mason Crest, 2007.

> Biography of rapper, actor, and Grammy-award winner Cornell Haynes Jr., better known as Nelly.

Hughes, Langston, editor. *The Best Short Stories by Black Writers: The Classic Anthology from 1899 to 1967.* Boston: Little, Brown, 1967.

> Langston Hughes's classic selection of short stories by African American writers.

Juzwiak, Richard. *LL Cool J.* Hip-Hop Biographies series. New York: Rosen Publishing Group, 2006.

> This edition looks at the life and career of James Todd Smith, better known to the world as LL Cool J.

Live Your Best Life: A Treasury of Wisdom, Wit, Advice, Interviews and Inspiration from O. By the editors of *O: The Oprah Magazine.* Birmingham, AL: Oxmoor House, 2005.

> From the popular television personality Oprah Winfrey, a compilation of words of wisdom about living life to the fullest. Teens will enjoy.

Seymour, Gene. *Jazz, the Great American Art.* New York: Franklin Watts, 1995.

> Jazz has been called the first uniquely American art form. This innovative and creative style of music was largely invented and shaped by African American musicians. This book traces the history of jazz back to its roots in blues, ragtime, and swing music.

Simone, Jacquelyn. *OutKast.* Hip-Hop series. Broomall, PA: Mason Crest, 2008.

> Biography of the hip-hop group OutKast.

Stewart, Mark. *Will Smith.* Star Files series. Chicago: Raintree, 2005.

> This biography covers the life of Will Smith from his childhood and early days as the Fresh Prince in the hip-hop duo DJ Jazzy Jeff and the Fresh Prince, to his impressive rise to fame as one of the most successful actors in Hollywood.

Torres, Jennifer. *Mary J. Blige.* A Blue Banner Biography. Hockessin, DE: Mitchell Lane Publishers, 2008.

> This brief biography examines the life of Mary J. Blige from her childhood in New York City to her stellar success in the 1990s.

Torres, John Albert. *P. Diddy.* A Blue Banner Biography. Hockessin, DE: Mitchell Lane Publishers, 2005.

> A biography of Sean John Combs, successful rap musician, music producer, fashion designer, and entrepreneur.

Vibe Magazine. *Hip-hop divas.* New York: Three Rivers Press, 2001.

> Short biographies of popular female entertainers, including Lauryn Hill, Mary J. Blige, and hip-hop group TLC.

Winchell, Donna Haisty. *Alice Walker.* Twayne's United States Author Series. New York: Twayne Publishers, 1992.

> This work of literary criticism focuses on the work of Alice Walker. While a brief biography is included, the focus of this work is on the critical interpretation of Walker's writing. Includes chronology and annotated bibliography. Suitable for high school or college students.

Wittmann, Kelly. *Sean "Diddy" Combs.* Hip-Hop series. Bloomall, PA: Mason Crest, 2007.

> A biography of Sean John Combs, successful rap musician, music producer, fashion designer, and entrepreneur.

Woog, Adam. *Ray Charles and the Birth of Soul.* Lucent Library of African American History. Detroit, MI: Lucent Books, 2006.

> This biography looks at the life of one of the most popular and successful musicians in pop music.

African American Sports Stars

Aaseng, Nathan. *African-American Athletes.* A to Z of African Americans series. New York: Facts on File, 2003.

> This volume focuses on professional and amateur athletes of the twentieth century. It covers more than 150 athletes in just over 250 pages.

Abdul-Jabbar, Kareem, and Alan Steinberg. *Black Profiles in Courage: A Legacy of African American Achievement.* New York: William Morrow, 1996.

> Explores the legacy of courageous African Americans. While many of the stories offered here are about African Americans who stood up to overwhelming odds, Abdul-Jabbar also includes notable Africans like Cinque, who led the mutiny aboard the Amistad, and Estevanico, who was the first African to see the lands that would become Arizona and New Mexico.

Ashe, Arthur R., Jr. *A Hard Road to Glory: A History of the African American Athlete; Baseball.* New York: HarperCollins/Amistad, 1993.

> A substantial history of the African American athlete written and compiled by one of America's greatest athletes.

George, Nelson. *Elevating the Game: Black Men and Basketball.* New York: HarperCollins, 1992.

> Explores the role of African Americans in shaping the game of basketball.

The book also looks at how the game of basketball has shaped the identity and aspirations of young black men.

Gilbert, Thomas W. *Baseball and the Color Line.* The African-American Experience series. New York: Franklin Watts, 1995.

This book spends a lot of time looking at American sports in the nineteenth century before the color line became so rigid, identifying many African American sports firsts. Includes archival photos and appendixes.

Grolier Educational. *Pro Sports Halls of Fame.* Danbury, CT: Grolier Educational, 1996.

Multivolume reference set that focuses on athletes who have been inducted into the football, baseball, basketball, and hockey halls of fame. Includes biographies, career statistics, and special achievements.

Jordan, Roslyn, and Deloris Jordan. Illus. by Kadir Nelson. *Salt in His Shoes: Michael Jordan in Pursuit of a Dream.* New York: Simon and Schuster Books for Young Readers, 2000.

Confronted with doubts about his ability to play basketball, a young Michael Jordan learns some important lessons from his parents about determination, patience, and hard work.

Mattern, Joanne. *Basketball Greats.* History Makers series. San Diego: Lucent Books, 2003.

Solid biographies relying on primary source material. Profiles six notable players who helped change the sport.

Nelson, Kadir. *We Are the Ship: The Story of Negro League Baseball.* New York: Hyperion/Jump at the Sun, 2008.

Nelson's history of the Negro League details its inception in the 1920s through the league's demise after Jackie Robinson integrated Major League Baseball. Oil paintings by Nelson illustrate the compelling story.

Plowden, Martha Ward. Illus. by Ronald Jones. *Olympic Black Women.* Gretna, LA: Pelican Publishing, 1996.

A historical time line and biographical sketches bring to life black female Olympic athletes. Covers 1932 to the early 1990s.

Price, Sean. *Jackie Robinson: Breaking the Color Barrier.* Chicago: Raintree Fusion, 2009.

Details the life of Jackie Robinson from his youth, to his moment as the first African American to play in Major League Baseball, to his years after baseball. A marvelous introduction on how to use primary source material for historical research.

Scientific Achievements from African Americans

Graham, Shirley, and George Lipscomb. Illus. by Elton C. Fax. *Dr. George Washington Carver, Scientist.* New York: Julian Messner Publishing, 1944.

A classic biography about this important African American scientist.

Jones, Lynda. Illus. by Ron Garnett. *Five Brilliant Scientists.* Great Black Heroes series. New York: Scholastic, 2000.

Sketches the early life and major accomplishments of Susan McKinney Steward, George Washington Carver, Ernest Everett Just, Percy Lavon Julian, and Shirley Ann Jackson.

Schraff, Anne E. *Charles Drew: Pioneer in Medicine.* Berkeley Heights, NJ: Enslow Publishers, 2003.

A biography of the African American doctor noted for his pioneering work with blood transfusions.

Spangenburg, Ray, Kit Moser, and Diane Moser. *African Americans in Science, Math, and Invention.* A to Z of African Americans series. New York: Facts on File, 2003.

This volume profiles one hundred and sixty notable scientists from 1731 to the present day.

Sullivan, Otha Richard. *African American Women Scientists and Inventors.* Black Stars series. New York: Wiley, 2002.

Short biographies of twenty-five African American women who have made significant contributions to science. Explains the important contributions made despite widespread societal indifference. This book is a welcome effort to give these women some of the recognition they deserve.

Wellman, Sam. *George Washington Carver: Inventor and Naturalist.* Urichsville, OH: Barbour Publishing, 1998.

The story of the man who revolutionized agriculture in the southern United States. Carver was a scientist, educator, botanist, and inventor.

Important African American Women

Allen, Zita. *Black Women Leaders of the Civil Rights Movement.* Danbury, CT: Franklin Watts, 1996.

Examines the role played by African American women in the civil rights movement from the turn of the century to the civil rights legislation of the 1960s. This book works to rectify the oversight of these brave women, who were often ignored by historians.

Bloom, Harold. *Maya Angelou.* Philadelphia: Chelsea House, 1998.

Critical literary guide to the work of Maya Angelou. This examination of Angelou's work includes a chronology, bibliography, and introductory essay by Harold Bloom, one of the foremost literary critics of our age.

Bloom, Harold. *Maya Angelou's I Know Why the Caged Bird Sings.* Philadelphia: Chelsea House, 1998.

A close examination of the themes and structure of Angelou's most famous work. Includes index of themes and ideas found in this remarkable book.

Coddon, Karin S. *Black Women Activists.* San Diego: Greenhaven Press, 2004.

Looks at eight women from around the world who have fought for black freedom. Includes both historical figures like Sojourner Truth and contemporary figures like Winnie Mandela. Includes an appendix of primary source documents.

Colbert, David. *Michelle Obama: An American Story.* **Boston: Houghton Mifflin, 2009.**

Covers the history of the first lady's family as much as the story of her youth. This is the story of a family that, over generations, moved from slavery to the White House.

Olson, Lynne. *Freedom's Daughters: The Unsung Heroines of the Civil Rights Movement from 1830 to 1970.* **New York: Scribner, 2001.**

This wide-ranging, comprehensive history of women in the civil rights movement stretches back to the 1830s, and up to the 1970s.

Schraff, Anne E. *Coretta Scott King: Striving for Civil Rights.* **Springfield, NJ: Enslow Publishers, 1997.**

This biography of civil rights leader Coretta Scott King looks at her life from her childhood in Alabama to her lifelong efforts to help the underprivileged and her leadership in the fight against inequality in all of its forms.

Fiction/Poetry

Adams, Lenora. *Baby Girl.* **New York: Simon and Schuster/Simon Pulse, 2007.**

Tough, pregnant Sheree explains in a letter to her mother why she's left home. Teens may relate to the difficulties Sheree faces with her family and friends.

Anderson, M. T. *The Astonishing Life of Octavian Nothing, Traitor to the Nation, Vol. 1: The Pox Party.* **Cambridge, MA: Candlewick, 2006.**

Anderson, M. T. *The Astonishing Life of Octavian Nothing, Traitor to the Nation, Vol. 2: The Kingdom on the Waves.* **Cambridge, MA: Candlewick, 2008.**

During the American Revolution, Octavian is raised as a pampered African prince by a society of Enlightenment philosophers who view him as an experiment. Realizing that his freedom is an illusion, Octavian sets off on a journey to find freedom and a place in the world. These books will challenge everything you have ever learned about the Revolutionary War. Respectively, the two books are 2007 and 2009 Michael L. Printz Honor Books.

Booth, Coe. *Kendra.* **New York: PUSH, 2008.**

Kendra is thrilled that her mom, Renee, has completed her PhD program—now they can finally be a real family. But is Renee excited for their future together, too?

Brooks, Bruce. *The Moves Make the Man: A Novel.* **New York: Harper and Row, 1984.**

The story of a friendship between two boys, one white, one black, each with his own challenges to face, and a shared love for basketball. 1985 Newbery Honor Book.

Draper, Sharon M. *Forged by Fire.* **New York: Atheneum Books for Young Readers, 1997.**

The story of a troubled teen in a dysfunctional family working to protect his beloved half-sister from their abusive father. A realistic portrait of child abuse and the challenges of poverty.

Draper, Sharon M. *Tears of a Tiger.* **New York: Atheneum Books for Young Readers, 1994.**

When high school basketball star Rob Washington dies in a car accident, the lives of many are changed—perhaps most of all, the life of Andy, who was driving the car on that fatal trip.

Hughes, Langston. Illus. by Romare Bearden. *The Block: Poems.* **New York: Viking, 1995.**

This collection of thirteen poems by Langston Hughes celebrates the New York City neighborhood of Harlem. Hughes's celebratory poetry is illustrated by the collage painting of Romare Bearden.

Johnson, Angela. *The First Part Last.* **New York: Simon and Schuster Books for Young Readers, 2003.**

On his sixteenth birthday Bobby learns that his girlfriend is pregnant and he is about to become a father. Bobby must suddenly face adult decisions and figure out the right thing to do. Winner of the 2004 Michael L. Printz Award for Excellence in Young Adult Literature.

Lipsyte, Robert. *The Contender.* **New York: Harper and Row, 1967.**

This classic work tells the story of a young man who drops out of high school and avoids street gangs by spending time at the gym. He learns that dreams of being a contender don't come easy. Lipsyte was honored for this book, and others, with a 2001 Margaret A. Edwards Award.

Myers, Walter Dean. *Hoops.* **New York: Delacorte, 1981.**

This is the tale of a friendship between a young basketball player and a disgraced professional player who tries to prevent others from making the same mistakes he did.

Myers, Walter Dean. *The Outside Shot.* **New York: Delacorte, 1984.**

Moving from Harlem to a college in the Midwest is challenge enough, but finding his way through the corruption in college sports makes the transition even tougher.

Naylor, Gloria, ed. *Children of the Night: The Best Short Stories by Black Writers, 1967 to the Present.* **Boston: Little, Brown, 1995.**

Thirty-seven great tales about the black experience. This book covers the last forty years of fiction by African American writers.

Woodson, Jacqueline. *After Tupac and D Foster.* **New York: G. P. Putnam's Sons, 2008.**

The friendship of three girls from very different families fills the emptiness of uncertainty as they struggle with Tupac Shakur's troubles as well as their own.

CHAPTER 2

Exploring Asian Cultures

Delightful Days of the Dragon: Celebrating Chinese New Year in Style

By Kimberly Craig

Age Level

12–18 years

Duration of Library Program

50–60 minutes per class or session

Introduction and Background

The celebration of the new year is an extremely lively and important holiday in China and, indeed, in Chinese communities worldwide. Traditionally, it marks the beginning of the planting season in China. Chinese New Year occurs annually in late January or early February and is determined by the Chinese lunar calendar. The holiday traditionally lasts for fifteen days, although due to busy schedules, many modern families limit the festivities to five days.

The most popular event during Chinese New Year is the enormous parade featuring fireworks, dancing lions, and a gargantuan dragon. The dragon is made up of a huge dragon mask worn by one person and a long, brightly colored body carried by many dancers hidden beneath the material. The Eastern dragon, which is quite different from its Western counterpart, is a focal point of both the parade and the holiday as a whole because it is considered to be a bringer of rain and good luck, important during the planting season.

In the United States, Chinese New Year festivities are held in San Francisco and New York City, as well as in other locations with large pockets of Chinese Americans. By celebrating this popular Chinese holiday at your school and in your library, you will help students learn about Chinese culture and customs, with a particular emphasis on the lore surrounding Eastern dragons.

Overall Goal

The students will celebrate Chinese New Year in a cross-curricular event that will enhance their understanding of Chinese culture in general and of Chinese New Year in particular.

The library program helps students to gain an understanding and appreciation of the significance and importance of dragons as they relate to traditional Chinese culture.

Relevance to the Community Served

The event will help students gain valuable insight into the rich cultural heritage of China, and the library's program in particular will help them make the connection between literature and traditional Chinese beliefs about dragons.

Activities

The Chinese New Year celebration can easily become a schoolwide event. For example, students can create Chinese paper lanterns in art class, study the Chinese zodiac in science class, engage in various Chinese games in math class, read Chinese poetry in English class, watch a video of a real Chinese New Year festival in social studies class, eat traditional Chinese food for lunch, and so on. These activities can be adapted as appropriate.

The day will culminate with a big Chinese New Year party, and students will have the opportunity to show off all that they have done and experienced earlier in the day.

The activities that occur during the library program involve learning about Eastern dragons and their importance to Chinese culture through select readings, comparing Eastern dragons with their Western counterparts, and showing specific examples of what Eastern dragons look like.

As a media center activity, a brief history of the immigration of the Chinese to the United States will be presented. The Chinese American culture will be introduced by highlighting the Chinese New Year celebration. The traditions, superstitions, and folklore of the celebration will also be addressed.

Prior to Chinese New Year, students will read the novel *Dragonwings* by Laurence Yep in their literature classes, and they will discuss it in depth. In addition, in their social studies classes, they will discuss life as it was for Chinese immigrants to the United States in the early 1900s and life as it is for them now. Also, in social studies classes, they will discuss the meaning and significance of major Chinese holidays, including Chinese New Year.

Sample Schedule of Events

- Welcome students to the library's portion of the Chinese New Year festivities
- Introduce the topic of Chinese dragons to the students
- Explore selected materials dealing with Eastern dragons
- Discuss cultural and historical aspects of the book *Dragonwings*
- Compare Chinese dragons with those from Western cultures
- Discuss why dragons are so important in Chinese folklore
- Show examples of what Chinese dragons look like
- Give out *lai see* envelopes as take-away prizes
- Distribute annotated bibliographies for those seeking to learn more

Preparation

Just before the schoolwide Chinese New Year celebration, promotional letters will be distributed to the relevant homeroom teachers for students to take home. Other fliers will be displayed in prominent areas in classrooms and near the library. These letters and fliers can advertise the entire celebration, not just the library's portion of the program.

The library itself will be decorated for the occasion with red and gold balloons, red streamers, red couplets written in gold ink hanging on long banners, and *lai see* envelopes (each containing a little gift) for take-away prizes.

In preparation for the library's program, the librarian will select material to share with the students dealing with dragons in general and with Eastern dragons in particular. This material will include descriptions of dragons, images of dragons, stories about dragons, and so on. The librarian will create an annotated bibliography of dragon lore to take home.

Cost and Materials

Approximate cost: $10–$50

- Chinese New Year decorations such as red and gold balloons, red streamers, and red couplets (good-luck sayings written on red paper) to hang in the library
- *Lai see* envelopes (red envelopes with little gifts inside, given for good luck)
- Selected literature and printouts from a variety of sources
- Pictures of dragons

Bibliography

Bouchard, Dave. Illus. by Zhong-Yang Huang. *The Dragon New Year: A Chinese Legend.* Atlanta, GA: Peachtree, 1999.
    A blend of fact and folklore explaining how Chinese New Year traditions came to be.

Chambers, Catherine. *Chinese New Year.* Austin, TX: Raintree Steck-Vaughn, 1997.
    An introduction to the ceremonies, traditions, and foods that go along with the celebration of Chinese New Year.

Cheong, Colin. *China.* Edited by Elizabeth Berg. Milwaukee, WI: Gareth Stevens Publishing, 1997.
    Tells the story of China through its many festivals.

Daley, William. *The Chinese Americans.* Philadelphia: Chelsea House, 1996.
    A look at why Chinese immigrated to North America, and their acceptance as an ethnic group. Also looks at Chinese culture, history, and religion, and the factors that drove some to seek a home in a new land.

Duane, O. B., and N. Hutchison. *Chinese Myths and Legends.* London: Brockhampton Press, 1998.
    A collection of some of the most intriguing mythological tales from ancient China.

Moy, Tina. *Chinese Americans.* New York: Marshall Cavendish, 1995.
    Information about China, why people immigrated to America, and their reception once they got to the United States.

Robinson, Fay. *Chinese New Year: A Time for Parades, Family, and Friends.* Finding Out about Holidays series. Berkeley Heights, NJ: Enslow Publishers, 2001.

Origin of the Chinese New Year and how it is celebrated in the United States and around the world.

Sanders, Tao Tao Liu. Illus. by Johnny Pau. *Dragons, Gods and Spirits from Chinese Mythology.* New York: P. Bedrick Books, 1995.

A compilation of Chinese stories full of dragons and spirits. The work includes myths, folktales, religious legends, and popular superstitions.

Yep, Laurence. *Dragonwings.* New York: Harper and Row, 1975.

A historical novel about a Chinese boy and his father who immigrate to the United States in 1903.

Zhang, Song Nan, and Hao Yu Zhang. *A Time of Golden Dragons.* Toronto: Tundra Books, 2000.

A beautiful book that commemorates the year of the Golden Dragon by tracing Chinese dragon history and introducing Chinese dragon legends.

Webliography

American Museum of Natural History. "Dragons: Creatures of Power." www.amnh.org/exhibitions/mythiccreatures/dragons/.

Examine the characteristics of Chinese and European dragons and learn about their magical powers. Uncover how dinosaur fossils helped to keep dragon legend alive.

China the Beautiful. "Dragons in Ancient China." www.chinapage.com/dragon1.html.

View numerous photographs of Chinese architecture, paintings, and cultural items embellished with symbols of dragons.

Newton Public Schools. "Dragons." www.newton.k12.ma.us/Angier/DimSum/Dragon%20Pictures.html.

Study how a Chinese dragon really looks while viewing these superb examples of dragon art.

San Francisco Chinatown Merchants Association. "The Legend of the Chinese Dragon." www.moonfestival.org/legends/dragon.htm.

Compare western dragon folklore with eastern dragon folklore, learn the profile of the Chinese dragon, and study its appearance and its role in Chinese parades and calendars.

A Road to India

By Linda Alexander and Nahyun Kwon

Age Level
14–18 years

Duration of Library Program
3 hours for each event

Introduction and Background
Watching movies is a favorite pastime of the Indian people. The program on India will consist of watching popular Indian movies on Friday nights. Watching movies is a great way to experience the culture and life of Indians and Indian Americans. The entertainment and educational program can be held as part of the library's wider Asian Pacific Heritage Month in May.

Overall Goal

This event will encourage teens to enjoy movies in the library's teen space and will aid comprehension about the ways that young people of Indian origin live.

Relevance to the Community Served

Young adults tend to know very little about actual Indian history, tradition, customs, family and social life, and pop culture. This program of movies and books will serve to broaden the teen's understanding of the culture.

Activities

The librarian will have pulled popular titles for a display on books on the theme of the Indian culture. (Suggested books for a display can be found in the bibliography.) Teen volunteers from your teen advisory group (TAG) can arrive fifteen to twenty minutes early to prepare microwave popcorn and distribute pizza and soda for all attendants. They can be in charge of getting the movie started.

When the movie is over, the teen librarian or the TAG can lead discussion about the movie. The librarian can distribute the handout of book titles, and participants may check out books as they leave.

Preparation

The event will be advertised primarily through word-of-mouth by the librarians either at the library or while doing outreach to the local schools. Also, a flier will be created by the programming coordinator to be distributed to patrons within the library, posted on the library's website, and mailed out with event packages to the schools.

A member of the TAG will have volunteered to read and prepare a movie talk for this Friday night event. A movie will be chosen from the list. (See the bibliography.) Microwave popcorn, soda, and pizza can be purchased in advance.

Cost and Materials

Approximate cost: $30 for twenty participants

- Fliers to advertise event
- Movie
- Handouts showing book titles
- Food: popcorn, soda, pizza

Bibliography

Books

Aikath-Gyaltsen, Indrani. *Daughters of the House.* New York: Random House, 1994.
> A complicated story of passion and betrayal among a family of women in rural India.

Bosse, Malcolm J. *Tusk and Stone.* Arden, NC: Front Street, 1995.
> Set in India in the seventh century, this is the story of Arjun, a young Brahman who is sold into slavery, becomes a soldier, and finally discovers his true talents as a sculptor.

Desai Hidier, Tanuja. *Born Confused.* New York: Scholastic Press, 2002.
> A coming-of-age story about Dimple, who is torn between her Indian heritage and her life in America, not seeming to fit into either.

Divakaruni, Chitra Banarjee. *Mistress of Spices.* New York: Anchor Books, 1998.
> Novel about Tilo's choice of a life of special powers in spices over an ordinary life in India.

Divakaruni, Chitra Banarjee. *Neela, Victory Song.* Girls of Many Lands/American Girls series. Middleton, WI: Pleasant Company, 2002.
> Novel about a twelve-year-old Indian girl in 1939 during India's struggle for freedom against British rule.

Galbraith, Catherine Atwater, and Rama Mehta. *India, Now and Through Time.* Boston: Houghton Mifflin, 1980.
> Overview of India's history, culture, land, and people.

Kipling, Rudyard. *The Jungle Book.* New York: Puffin Classics, 2006.
> Mowgli grows up in the jungles of India with help from the animals, but has not yet faced the ferocious Bengal tiger.

Lahiri, Jhumpa. *The Namesake.* Boston: Houghton Mifflin, 2003.
> The multigenerational story of a family with roots in the east and a life in the west. Well-drawn characters provide insight into the challenges of the immigrant experience, while celebrating the diversity of the sometimes conflicting cultures.

McDaniel, Jan. *Indian Immigration.* The Changing Face of North America series. Philadelphia: Mason Crest, 2004.
> Overview of immigration from India to the United States and Canada since the 1960s.

Murari, Timeri. *Field of Honor: A Novel.* New York: Simon and Schuster, 1981.
> The story of an American boxer who is stranded in Bangalore, where he lives with the Anglo-Indian community.

Rana, Indi. *The Roller Birds of Rampur.* New York: Henry Holt and Company, 1993.
> The story of a teenager raised in England who returns to India to discover her roots.

Sheth, Kashmira. *Blue Jasmine.* **New York: Hyperion Books for Children, 2004.**

Fictional tale of twelve-year-old Jasmine, who leaves her native India with her family to settle in Iowa City.

Sundaresan, Indu. *The Twentieth Wife: A Novel.* **New York: Washington Square Press, 2003.**

Fictionalized account of the life of Mehrunnisa, a sixteenth-century empress of India whose love helped shape the course of the Mughal empire in the seventeenth century.

Whelan, Gloria. *Homeless Bird.* **New York: HarperCollins, 2000.**

Bound to a forced marriage, then widowed while still young, Koly sets out to create a life for herself in a strange city.

Yapp, Malcolm. *Gandhi.* **Farmington Hills, MI: Greenhaven Press, 1980.**

Overview of historical events of India, Gandhi's life history and his beliefs and values.

Yolen, Jane. *Children of the Wolf.* **New York: Puffin Books, 1993.**

In 1920 in India two children who have been raised by wolves are discovered and brought to an orphanage to be taught human behavior again.

Movies

Bend It Like Beckham. **2003. With Gurinder Chadha, Deepak Nayar, Guljit Bindra, Paul Mayeda Berges, Parminder Nagra, Keira Knightley, Jonathan Rhys-Meyers, et al.**

Jessmindar dreams of becoming a professional football player in England, her idol being David Beckham. But her Punjabi parents push her toward academics so she will end up being financially successful. Who will win the struggle?

Mississippi Masala. **2003. With Michael Nozik, Mira Nair, Sooni Taraporevala, Denzel Washington, Sarita Choudhury, Roshan Seth, Sharmila Tagore, et al.**

Romance turns to turmoil when an Indian daughter, who is the maid at her family's motel in Greenwood, Mississippi, falls for a local African American carpet cleaner (Denzel Washington). The two families cannot accept this. Very comical.

Monsoon Wedding. **2002. With Mira Nair, Caroline Baron, Sabrina Dhawan, Naseeruddin Shah, Lillete Dubey, Shefali Shetty, Vijay Raaz, Tilotama Shome, Vasundhara Das, and Kulbhushan Kharbanda.**

Aditi does not want to marry the man she hardly knows, but her father has arranged a traditional Punjabi wedding in Delhi. All the relatives will attend; there are many comical romantic problems in the four days covered in the movie.

Slumdog Millionaire. 2008. With Christian Colson, Simon Beaufoy, Loveleen Tandan, Danny Boyle, Dev Patel, Anil Kapoor, Saurabh Shukla, et al. Winner of eight Academy Awards, this movie portrays an eighteen-year-old Indian slum kid who plays on the Indian version of the TV show *Who Wants to Be a Millionaire?* He has the chance to win millions of rupees, but there are questions about his honesty. Did he cheat?

Webliography

Festivals in India. www.festivalsinindia.net.

The Library of Congress. "A Country Study India." http://lcweb2.loc.gov/frd/cs/intoc.html.

1,000 Cranes—Origami Day

By Patricia M. Jankowski

Age Level
12–14 years

Duration of Library Program
60 minutes

Overall Goal

This program is designed for a media center in a middle school. The school's curriculum includes multicultural themes, and all grades study the same culture at the same time. The origami program in the media center will take place when the school is studying Japan.

The overall goal is to use origami, teach peace, and open the door to further appreciation of and learning about Japanese culture. At the end of this program, students will be able to provide a definition for origami, create origami cranes, explain the cultural relevance of origami cranes, and explain who Sadako is and why her story is important.

Relevance to the Community Served

This program relates to the middle school social science curriculum and to paper cranes as represented in a "World Peace" event held each year by the school.

Activities

All classes will visit the media center over a one- or two-day period. The students will already be familiar with the story of Sadako Sasaki, a young cancer patient who folded more than a thousand paper cranes in the name of world peace. The media specialist will reinforce the story by reading the book *Sadako,* by Eleanor Coerr. There should be a question-and-answer period afterward, and then the students will make paper cranes. The goal of the program is for the school to create one thousand cranes and mail them to Hiroshima to be placed on the statue of Sadako. (Teachers and the media specialist will string the cranes on garlands of one hundred, as requested by the city of Hiroshima.)

> Mailing address:
> Office of the Mayor
> City of Hiroshima
> 6-34 Kokutaiji-Machi
> 1 Chome Naka-ku, Hiroshima 730
> Japan

While the children are folding, play Japanese music.

After each student folds four or more cranes, have a second question-and-answer period, followed by very brief booktalks on fiction and nonfiction books related to origami, Sadako, Japan, etc.

Preparation

Prior to Origami Day, familiarize students with the story of Sadako Sasaki, as well as some basic information about origami. In addition to the books listed, the media specialist should pull books about Japan, peace, cranes, paper crafts, etc. and have them on display, accessible to the children.

Cost and Materials

Approximate cost: $0–$20

- Origami paper
- Shipping
- Music

Bibliography

Coerr, Eleanor. Illus. by Ronald Himler. *Sadako and the Thousand Paper Cranes.*
New York: Puffin, 1999.
Legend says that if a person folds one thousand paper cranes, her wish will
come true. A child in Hiroshima, hospitalized with leukemia brought on by
radiation fallout from the atom bomb, races against time to make the legend
come true.

Costain, Meredith, and Paul Collins. *Welcome to Japan.* Broomall, PA: Chelsea
House, 2002.
Excellent resource with short but interesting information on a variety of
topics that range from Japanese family life to industry and agriculture. Great
color photographs.

Galvin, Irene Flum. *Japan: A Modern Land with Ancient Roots.* Exploring Cultures of the World series. Tarrytown, NY: Benchmark Books, 1996.
This book provides more in-depth information about Japan and the Japanese way of life: geography and history; people; family life; festivals and
food; school and recreation; and the arts. It includes an excellent section on
ancient traditions and a succinct section on country facts, as well as a glossary and suggestions for further reading. Color photographs.

Hamanaka, Sheila. *Screen of Frogs: An Old Tale.* New York: Orchard Books, 1993.
A humorous tale about lazy man who learns to appreciate the rewards of
hard work and the beautiful things around him.

Kitano, Harry H. L. *The Japanese Americans.* New York: Chelsea House, 1987.
Discusses Japanese immigration to the United States, including the historical context in the 1860s, the different generations of Japanese American, the
wartime evacuation, and the Japanese American contributions. Color and
black-and-white pictures.

McAlpine, Helen, and William McAlpine. Illus. by Rosamund Fowler. *Tales
from Japan.* New York: Oxford University Press, 2002.
A collection of fairy tales and legends from Japan. These folktales and
magical characters evoke the magic and enchantment of a people and their
landscape.

Shelley, Rex, Teo Chuu Yong, and Russell Mok. *Japan.* New York: Marshall Cavendish, 2002.
Excellent, in-depth, and very comprehensive resource on all relevant
aspects pertaining to Japan: geography, history, government, economy,
lifestyle, etc. Great sections on the arts and festivals. Many color photographs.

Temko, Florence. Illus. by Randall Gooch. *Traditional Crafts from Japan.* Culture Crafts series. Minneapolis, MN: Lerner, 2001.
Clear instructions and great illustrations for easy-to-make, traditional Japanese crafts such as origami and stenciled fabrics.

Webliography

Ashliman, D. L., ed. "Folktales from Japan." www.pitt.edu/~dash/japan.html.
  Compilation of Japanese folktales.

Japanese American National Museum. www.janm.org.
  The Japanese American National Museum is dedicated to sharing the experience of Americans of Japanese ancestry.

Library of Congress. "Country Study of Japan." http://lcweb2.loc.gov/frd/cs/jptoc.html.
  Detailed information about the country of Japan.

UCLA Center for East Asian Studies. "Teaching about Japan." www.international.ucla.edu/eas/japan/lessons/introduction.htm.
  Resource providing links to information on various aspects of Japanese culture.

Morikami Museum and Gardens. www.morikami.org.
  The Morikami Museum and Japanese Gardens in Palm Beach County, Florida, is a center for Japanese arts and culture.

Thousand Cranes Peace Network. http://rosella.apana.org.au/~mlb/cranes/index.htm.
  An international network connecting people and activities that promote peace, nonviolence, and tolerance.

Learning Japanese Culture through Manga

By Kimberly DeFusco and Alex Hernandez

Age Level
13–18 years

Duration of Library Program
2 hours

Introduction and Background

Many libraries have popular manga and anime clubs, as well as high circulation rates of manga and anime. A day of Japanese cultural activities is a great way to supplement our young patrons' diet of Japanese pop culture with a deeper look at the more long-lived aspects of Japanese culture and traditions. Students will identify cultural values and ideals demonstrated in Japanese comics, support their findings by citing examples from Japanese comics, compare and contrast these values to their own culture using graphic organizers, and appreciate how art can contribute to the development and transmission of culture, and lead to a greater cross-cultural understanding.

A speaker from the Japanese community will give a talk about the culture of Japan.

Overall Goal

Although the library's young adults consume a large amount of popular Japanese material, they know very little about actual Japanese history, customs, and traditions. This program will offer students insight into how to use their passion for manga and their critical thinking skills to learn about Japanese culture through reading.

Relevance to the Community Served

Participants in this program are voracious readers of manga. This program will enhance their knowledge and enjoyment of the Japanese culture by using their interest in manga.

Activities

Cosplay

The term *cosplay* refers to the practice of anime and manga fans to dress up as their favorite characters, usually in homemade costumes. Participants are encouraged, but not required, to dress up.

Guest Lecturer

The guest lecturer from the Japanese community will provide information on Japan's pop culture and the life of Japanese teens, followed by a question-and-answer period. Some of the misperceptions or stereotypical images held by participants can be discussed.

Analyzing Manga for Culture Clues

After the guest lecturer completes his or her presentation:

- Students divide into groups of three to four
- Each group is provided with three or four different manga books
- Students develop theories to answer, "What can we learn about Japanese culture by reading manga?" paying attention to aspects of the culture (family, love, fashion, food, friends, architecture).

- Students analyze manga and take notes in a graphic organizer, cite specific evidence, comparing and contrasting with their own culture.
- Using butcher paper and markers, student groups create a poster to present their findings to the workshop.
- Tape posters around the workshop area. Groups take turns presenting their findings and the guest lecturer facilitates discussion when appropriate.

Student Discussion Topics

- What themes occurred in more than one manga?
- What are the most popular manga themes?
- Were any of your findings contradictory or surprising? If so, why?

Optional ideas might include: Provide students with personal invitations to the Manga Making program, offered in the media center during lunch period over one week, Monday through Friday. This follow-up program will be done in conjunction with the art teacher and will focus on using the insight gained in this workshop to develop a manga story line, create a storyboard, write, edit, and illustrate a manga for publication and distribution through the media center.

Preparation

- Preview manga books or reviews to ensure age appropriateness of all titles
- Recruit a volunteer presenter from the Japanese community
- Publicize the program through a morning show, posters around school, and fliers on the graphic novels collection rack
- Create a sign-up list in the media center
- Send invitations to students the day before the event, reminding them of the program and to bring lunch
- Create a display of manga books (enough for one for each student)
- Print/copy enough worksheets, graphic organizers, and sample manga illustrations from the book by Duffy (see bibliography) and the online Japanese Culture exhibit Teenage Tokyo: Youth and Popular Culture in Japan, at the Boston Children's Museum (www.mfa.org).

Cost and Materials

Approximate cost: $0–$50

- Sample manga illustrations (using Teenage Tokyo exhibit site at www.mfa.org)
- Japanese manga books (see bibliography)
- Student worksheet for cultural analysis / graphic organizer
- Butcher paper (one sheet per group)
- Markers
- Tape
- Making Manga fliers and invitations

Bibliography

Clamp, Ray Yoshimoto, and Jamie S. Rich. *CLAMP School Detectives. Volume 1.* Los Angeles: Tokyopop, 2003.
  Nokoru, Suoh, and Akira form the CLAMP School Detectives Agency to protect the vulnerable and save the day.

Duffy, Jo. Illus. by Takashi Oguro. *Teenage Tokyo: The Story of Four Japanese Junior High School Students.* Boston: Children's Museum, 1990.
  Follow Mika (the shy girl), Kenji (the jock), Akiko (the fashionista), and Yuichi (the perfect, popular guy) through the challenges they must face as eighth graders at Tokyo Toyo Municipal Junior High School.

Hotta, Yumi, Takeshi Obata, and Yukari Umezawa. *Hikaru No Go. 1, Descent of the Go Master.* Shonen Jump Graphic Novel. San Francisco: VIZ Media, 2004.
  Hikaru Shindo is an average twelve-year-old boy until he awakens a thousand-year-old ghost living in a dusty old go game board in his grandfather's attic.

Konomi, Takeshi, Gerard Jones, and Andy Ristaino. *The Prince of Tennis. Vol. 7, St. Rudolph's Best.* Shonen Jump Graphic Novel. San Francisco: VIZ Media, 2005.
  Arrogant but talented tennis player Ryoma Echizen enrolls in Seishun Academy. However, on the road to nationals, Ryoma is matched against the "Lefty Killer." Can he keep his winning streak alive?

Miyazaki, Hayao. *My Neighbor Totoro. 1.* San Francisco: VIZ Media, 2004.
  After moving to an old house in the country, Satsuki and her sister discover an enchanted camphor tree, meet Granny and her grandson Kanta, experience the magic of Soot Sprites, and begin an adventure filled with mysterious creatures.

Miyazaki, Hayao, and Yuji Oniki. *Miyazaki's Spirited Away 5.* San Francisco: VIZ Media, 2002.
  While visiting a ghost town, Chihiro Ogino's parents are magically turned into pigs and she is made to work for the witch, Yubaba, at a spirit world bathhouse. She must change her name to Sen and seek the help of a mysterious but familiar boy named Haku in order to save her parents.

Nishiyama, Yuriko, Shirley Kubo, and Jordan Capell. *Rebound. Vol. 1*. Los Angeles: Tokyopop, 2003.

> Nate Torres doesn't think of himself as successful until he starts playing street basketball. At the National Basketball Championships in Sapporo, Nate's team realizes the competition is much tougher than the local Tokyo teams.

Sakai, Stan. *Usagi Yojimbo: Grasscutter*. Milwaukie, OR: Dark Horse Comics, 1999.

> Usagi finds "Grasscutter," a powerful sword, just as a demonic warrior, a Shogun samurai, and a witch are attempting to retrieve it. Can Usagi survive and prevent the evil emperor from regaining the throne?

Soda, Masahito, Lance Caselman, and Joe Yamazaki. *Firefighter! Daigo of Fire Company M. 1*. San Francisco: VIZ Media, 1996.

> Asahina Daigo is an eighteen-year-old new firefighter who quickly learns that the job is much more challenging than he originally thought. He must find the courage to be a hero, especially when he learns that his school enemy is working at a rival station.

Takahashi, Kazuki, Joe Yamazaki, and Rina Mapa. *Yu-Gi-Oh! Duelist. Vol. 2, The Puppet Master*. Shonen Jump Graphic Novel. San Francisco: VIZ Media, 2005.

> Yugi and friend Jonouchi must battle in the Duelist Kingdom to determine the greatest duel master.

Takahashi, Rumiko, and Mari Morimoto. *Inu Yasha. Vol. 4*. San Francisco: VIZ Media, 2003.

> Average schoolgirl Kagome realizes she's the reincarnated powerful priestess Kikyo, when she accidentally awakens the evil half-demon, Inu-Yasha, whom she had killed hundreds of years earlier. It is up to Kagome to save the world from him again.

Takaya, Natsuki. *Fruits Basket. Volume 1*. Los Angeles: Tokyopop, 2004.

> When orphan Tohru Honda is adopted by Yuki and Shigure Sohma (two bachelor cousins) she brightens their lives with her positive nature, until their sour and combative cousin, Kyo, arrives.

Takeuchi, Naoko. *Sailor Moon 1*. Los Angeles: Mixx Entertainment, 1998.

> Fourteen-year-old Usagi (Bunny in the English version) is changed forever when she meets Luna, a talking cat who gives her the power to turn into superhero Sailor Moon. Sailor Moon, teamed with Sailor Senshi, fight against attacking enemies and the evil power of Queen Beryl.

Tezuka, Osamu. *Astro Boy, 11*. Milwaukie, OR: Dark Horse Comics, 2002.

Tezuka, Osamu, and Frederik L. Schodt. *Astro Boy, 15*. Milwaukie, OR: Dark Horse Comics, 2003.

Tezuka, Osamu. *Astro Boy, 16*. Milwaukie, OR: Dark Horse Comics, 2003.

> Tensions continue as the robot population is denied true citizenship. As the robots prepares for revolt, the question persists: "Could robots truly have souls?" Atom (Astro Boy) must battle stereotypes, prejudice, human enemies, and even time to prevent the persecution of his race.

Tezuka, Osamu. *Black Jack.* **San Francisco: VIZ Media, 1998.**

Dr. Black Jack had a disfiguring accident as a child, which led to him becoming a talented and caring doctor. Too bad he's unlicensed, charges ridiculous amounts of money to help his patients, is hated by most, and has numerous enemies.

Toriyama, Akira. *Dragon Ball.* **San Francisco: VIZ Media, 2000.**

Goku and friends set out on a dangerous quest to recover seven Dragon Balls.

Tsuda, Masami. *Kare Kano: His and Her Circumstances. Volume 1.* **Los Angeles: Tokyopop, 2003.**

Soichiro Arima and Yukino Miyazawa are both attractive and popular high school students. And they both live double lives. Can their romance survive?

Yu, Yuen Wong. *Digital Digimon Monsters. Volume 4.* **Los Angeles: Tokyopop, 2003.**

While at summer camp, a group of seven, labeled the "digidestined," are magically transported into the digiworld. They must battle vampires and other monsters to return to Earth and find the key to victory—an eighth "digidestined" living somewhere in Tokyo.

Additional Materials

STUDENT WORKSHEET

Name _____   Group_____

As you review your manga books, pay close attention to pictures and dialogue that show Japanese cultural values and ideas. Take notes here. Be sure to indicate the manga title and page in the citation box.

FAMILY	LOVE	FASHION	OTHER
Citation	Citation	Citation	Citation
Compare/Contrast	Compare/Contrast	Compare/Contrast	Compare/Contrast

FOOD	SCHOOL LIFE	ARCHITECTURE	OTHER
Citation	Citation	Citation	Citation
Compare/Contrast	Compare/Contrast	Compare/Contrast	Compare/Contrast

Promoting Korean Literature and Culture

By Kate Dunigan Atlee

Age Level
15–16 years

Duration of Library Program
1-hour weekly program for four weeks

Overall Goal
This program aims to promote quality literature for teens on the theme of Korean Americans or Korean culture. The primary goal of this program is to introduce Korean and Korean American fiction to teens with the aim of helping them develop an appreciation and understanding of Korean culture.

Relevance to the Community Served
The theme of books on Korean American culture can be tied in with classes in history and language arts. This program is targeted at teens because

students in this age group are at an important stage in forming their cultural identity.

Activities

To strengthen the success of the program, it is best to secure the collaboration of history and language arts teachers. Along with promoting the program from the classroom and encouraging student attendance, teachers may agree to give students who attend the program extra credit points in their classes.

The program can take place each Friday of October during the lunch hour, when student participants will be invited to the library for book discussions or booktalks on Korean themes. The kickoff for the program can be the Friday closest to October third, which is an important holiday in Korea: National Foundation Day (*Kae Chun Jul*). National Foundation Day celebrates the founding of Korea in 2333 BC by Tan-gun (also spelled Tangun or Dangun).

In addition to hosting meetings on Fridays, the media specialist can put two or three trivia questions each week in the school's daily news announcements. Trivia questions will be about Korean sports, food, music, culture, and history. Trivia questions may be answered by all participants in this program as part of a contest.

A book display will be set up in the media center to highlight the library's Korean American book collection. Students will be invited to check out and read Korean books to share or booktalk with the group the following week. Korean parent volunteers can lend the library Korean objects (small pieces of art, photographs, fabric, traditional clothing, etc.) to add to the display.

A sample program:

1. First Friday: Program kickoff. The first Friday, introduce the program and its purpose. Discuss the Korean literature collection in the library and make sure students know where to find it. Direct students to the special display of Korean books and artifacts. Discuss the cultural and political history of South Korea by introducing the holiday National Foundation Day (*Kae Chun Jeol*), as well as two other national holidays: *Sam-Il Jeol* (March First, Independence Movement Day) and *Kwangbok-Jeol* (Independence Day). The media specialist could recommend Linda Sue Park's *When My Name Was Keoko* to students.

2. Second Friday: This week's theme will be myths and folklore. Students will be invited to talk about Korean myths, folktales, and fairy tales. Together, participants will read *The Korean Cinderella* by Shirley Climo and *The Rabbit's Escape* by Suzanne Crowder Han, and discuss their responses to the stories. A booktalk by the media specialist on a Korean folklore title can follow this discussion. Participants will check out any Korean title on the display, to be discussed the following week. A "dos and don'ts of booktalks" handout will be distributed. Among the dos are (1) prepare well, (2) present a wide variety of books, (3) organize the books to show as you talk, and (4) experiment with different formats. Some of the don'ts are (1) don't introduce books you have not read, (2) don't gush over a book—it will sell itself, (3) don't give literary criticism, and (4) don't tell the entire story.

3. Third Friday: This week's theme will be stereotypes and how they are promoted or dispelled in books about Korean Americans. What stereotypes do Koreans have about themselves? What stereotypes do non-Korean students have about Koreans? Discuss *F Is for Fabuloso* by Marie G. Lee. Students will booktalk other books by and about Korean Americans.

4. Fourth Friday: Last day of the program. A local tae kwon do instructor will be invited so that students will take a mini class in the Korean martial art that will help teens gain agility, balance, and discipline. Students will enjoy traditional Korean food on this last day of the program.

Preparation

In preparation for the event, promotional handouts and fliers will be created for distribution, student-made posters from the TAG can be displayed, books selections located, and the library decorated in colors with a Korean flag theme. An annotated bibliography of Korean literature will be prepared and distributed to participants as they leave. The librarian can seek community volunteers for display items, food, and a tae kwon do expert. It will help to get the teachers on board by providing information to them about the program in advance. If the program will not fit into lunch periods, the program can be scheduled so that all may participate.

Cost and Materials

Approximate cost: $0–$30 for food and prizes. The media specialist could solicit parent participation/donations.

- Promotional flier and handouts
- Trivia questions
- Korean food for final day of program
- Prizes for students who answer trivia questions
- Handout giving suggestions for booktalking

Bibliography

Climo, Shirley. Illus. by Ruth Heller. *The Korean Cinderella*. New York: Harper-
Collins, 1993.

> Pear Blossom takes on the familiar role of Cinderella in this Korean version
> of the classic fairy tale. A group of magical animals help her complete the
> impossible tasks laid out by her stepmother and help her find her true love.

Han, Suzanne Crowder. Illus. by Yumi Heo. *The Rabbit's Escape = Kusa Ilsaeng-
han t´okki*. New York: Henry Holt and Company, 1995.

> This bilingual book presents a traditional Korean folktale. The Dragon King
> of the East Sea falls ill and is told he will recover only if he eats a rabbit's
> liver. Once he learns why he has been brought to the king, Rabbit cleverly
> talks his way out of the situation, convincing the Dragon King that he left
> his liver on land. The rabbit is often a central character in Korean folklore.

Lee, Marie G. *F Is for Fabuloso*. New York: Avon Books, 1999.

> In this story everyone assumes that Jin-Ha must be good at math because
> Koreans are all geniuses, aren't they? This story deals realistically with the
> stereotype that all Asian American kids are super-smart students. Jin-Ha,
> whose family highly values education, lies to her mother about failing a
> math test, but manages to come clean in the end.

Lee, Marie G. *Necessary Roughness*. New York: HarperCollins, 1996.

> A pair of Korean twins encounters racism and struggles to fit in after moving
> to a small town in Minnesota from Los Angeles. This book also includes a
> sports theme.

Lee, Peter H. *Anthology of Korean Literature: From Early Times to the Nineteenth
Century*. UNESCO Collection of Representative Works. Honolulu: University Press of Hawaii, 1981.

> Comprehensive collection of Korean literature covering poetry and prose
> from the last fourteen hundred years. Includes biographies, myths, love
> poems, bucolic tales, and tales of wonder.

Lee, Peter H. *A History of Korean Literature*. Cambridge, UK: Cambridge University Press, 2003.

> This book is highly academic, but gives a thorough history of Korean litera-
> ture beginning in 682 when a royal Confucian academy was established in
> Korea and ending the discussion in the late twentieth century. Lee describes
> Korean literature as it developed, the importance of the "Confucian canon"
> up to the sociopolitical writings of the 1960s and 1970s. He includes a sec-
> tion on the literature of North Korea.

Mun, Nami. *Miles from Nowhere*. New York: Riverhead Books, 2009.

> Korean teenage runaway Joon is homeless on the streets of 1980s New York.
> (This book may be too mature for any but older teens.)

Na, An. *A Step from Heaven*. Asheville, NC: Front Street, 2001.

> This young adult book is about the acculturation experience of an immi-

grant Korean child on Ellis Island, who experiences an abusive father while growing from age four to womanhood.

Orban-Szontagh, Madeleine. *Traditional Korean Designs.* Dover Pictorial Archive Series. New York: Dover, 1991.

This book includes black-and-white line drawings inspired by authentic Korean arts and crafts dating from the first through the nineteenth centuries.

Park, Linda Sue. *Archer's Quest.* New York: Clarion Books, 2006.

The story of Korean history and lore with a twist of time-travel fantasy. Sixth-grader Kevin is home alone in Dorchester, New York, when an arrow flies through the air, pinning his baseball cap to the wall. A man claiming to be Koh Chu-mong, the great archer from a Korean kingdom in the first century BC, is only the first surprise.

Park, Linda Sue. *Project Mulberry.* New York: Clarion Books, 2005.

A seventh grader's family moves to a small town in Illinois, where they are the only Korean family in the neighborhood. Should she suggest to her buddy that raising silkworms be their science project?

Park, Linda Sue. *A Single Shard.* New York: Clarion Books, 2001.

This is the story of Tree-Ear, an orphan whose desire is to create celadon pottery, a trade passed only from father to son in twelfth-century Korea.

Park, Linda Sue. *When My Name Was Keoko.* New York: Clarion Books, 2002.

Sun-hee and her older brother Tae-yul live in Korea under Japanese rule in 1940. Korean customs and traditions are forbidden by law. As the family struggles under these conditions, all the dangers of World War II come to the region.

Yoo, Paula. *Good Enough.* New York: HarperCollins/HarperTeen, 2008.

Patti struggles to keep up with her immigrant Korean parents' expectations, while trying to be true to herself.

Webliography

Kim-Renaud, YoungKey, R. Richard Grinker, and Kirk W. Larsen, editors. (Washington, DC: Sigur Center for Asian Studies, 2004). "Korean American Literature." www.hawaii.edu/hivandaids/Korean_American_Literature.pdf

This collection of papers covers a variety of topics on Korean American literature. Some of the essays include "Roots and Wings: An Overview of Korean American Literature (1934–2003)" by Elaine H. Kim, "The Future of Korean American Literature" by Heinz Insu Fenkl, and "The Language of Stories" by Nora Okja Keller.

Korea.net. www.korea.net.

Official website of the Republic of Korea.

Smithsonian Asian Pacific American Program. "Curriculum Guide." www.apa.si.edu/Curriculum%20Guide-Final/index.htm.

This Smithsonian Institute website provides a brief description of Korean and Korean American history, literature, famous people, and lesson plans for teachers.

Teen life in South Korea. www.fiu.edu/~dwyere/teenlifeinkorea.html.

Cynthia Leitich Smith. "Korean and Korean American Children's and YA Books." www.cynthialeitichsmith.com/lit_resources/diversity/asian _am/korean.html.

This site is an excellent resource for finding Korean and Korean American books for children and young adults. Includes summaries and recommended age group for each title.

Additional Materials

SAMPLE TRIVIA QUESTIONS

(All information for trivia questions is taken from www.korea.net.)

What is the Korean flag called and what is the significance of its design?
(Answer: The Korean flag is called Taegeukgi. Its design symbolizes the principles of the yin and yang in Asian philosophy)

What is the highest mountain in Korea? (Answer: Baekdu-san)

What holiday do Koreans celebrate on October third?
(Answer: National Foundation Day)

What is doenjang? (Answer: soybean paste, a staple of the Korean diet)

When was the FIFA World Cup held in Seoul? (Answer: 2002)

How many Koreans are members of the Taekwondo Association?
(Answer: 3.8 million)

Which of the following companies is not Korean: Daewoo, Samsung, Sony, Hyundai, or LG Electronics? (Answer: Sony)

In 2007, which popular Korean singer/actor was named as one of *Time* magazine's "100 Most Beautiful People"? (Answer: Jeong Ji-hoon or "Rain")

What are the major religions in Korea?
(Answer: Christianity, Buddhism, and Confucianism)

What kind of fabric is Korea well known for producing and exporting?
(Answer: Silk)

Which country ruled over Korea during World War II? (Answer: Japan)

Celebrating Filipino American Culture

By Hal Harmon

Age Level
12–14 years

Duration of Library Program
Approximately 4 hours

Introduction and Background
With an estimated four million people of Filipino ancestry living in the United States, Filipino Americans make up one of America's largest Asian American populations. Yet because of Filipinos' high degree of assimilation, interracial marriage, and mixture of Spanish and American influence, they are often referred to as an "invisible minority." The Philippines has a long history of being ruled by foreign powers, most notably Spain and the United States. Because of this history, it is not uncommon for Filipinos to come to this country with a Spanish-sounding last name or already fluent in the English language. It is this diverse background and history that make Filipino Americans hard to categorize and often misunderstood.

Overall Goal

The purpose of this program is to shine some light on this "invisible" minority group. This program, geared to tweens and young teens, will ideally educate participants on several aspects of Filipino culture, including song, dance, food, and literature. Filipino American History Month is October and would be an opportune time to present this program.

Relevance to the Community Served

Many American youth are unfamiliar with the diverse background and culture of the Filipino people, even though they likely interact with them in school, sports, and other day-to-day activities. Filipino Americans are often lumped in with other Asian Americans or even Hispanic Americans and, as a result, are often overlooked as having their own unique culture. This program will open tweens' and teens' eyes to the rich culture of Filipino Americans.

Activities

First Hour: A Presentation on Filipino Culture

A local Filipino American resident or representative from a Filipino American community organization will discuss Filipino culture and traditions. During the presentation, the speaker will teach some basic words and phrases in Tagalog, the Filipino national language. At the end of the presentation, participants will have the opportunity to ask questions of the speaker.

Second Hour: Filipino Folktales and Reader's Theater

The librarian and interested participants will take turns reading Filipino folktales and stories from the titles *Filipino Children's Favorite Stories,* retold by Liana Romulo, and *Lakas and the Makibaka Hotel,* by Anthony D. Robles. The Romulo book is a collection of short, popular Filipino folktales. The Robles book, written in both English and Tagalog, is the story of a young boy and some new friends who struggle against a greedy landlord.

For the second part of the hour, there will be a reader's theater using the book *Tuko and the Birds: A Tale from the Philippines,* by Shirley Climo. This Filipino folktale tells the story of a peaceful coterie of birds who live in a house on top of Mount Pinatubo. Their harmonious songs bring peace to themselves and the villagers below. That harmony shatters when a pesky, loud gecko named Tuko moves in and creates discord among the birds and villagers. The birds must find a way to remove their unwanted guest and bring peace back to the village. Willing participants, using scripts and minor props, will bring this story to life.

Third Hour: An Authentic Filipino Lunch
Local Filipino American families will serve authentic Filipino cuisine to all participants. Some traditional dishes that may be presented include (but are not limited to)

> *Lumpias*—A thin Filipino eggroll, usually stuffed with meat and vegetables
> *Poncit*—A common Filipino dish of rice noodles mixed with vegetables and often a meat or seafood
> *Chicken Adobo*—often regarded as the national dish of the Philippines, chicken adobo consists of chicken cooked in vinegar and soy
> *Turon*—a banana fritter, usually served as a desert
> Plenty of rice, a staple of the Philippines

During lunch, traditional Filipino music will be sampled.

Fourth Hour: Philippine Folk Dance Demonstration
Local performers will demonstrate and teach a popular Filipino folk dance called "Tinikling." Also known as the bamboo dance, Tinikling involves pairs of people holding parallel bamboo poles. They tap the poles on the ground, then bring them together in a repetitive motion. As the poles are continuously moving, one or two people dance in between the poles. The dance takes skill and coordination. After the demonstration, participants will get a chance to try out the dance with instruction.

Preparation
Promotional fliers will be available in-house and distributed to local schools and community centers. Ads will be placed in local print and Internet resources (e.g., local calendar of events, local websites, and local newspapers). The librarian will solicit the expertise of a bamboo dancer, a speaker of the Tagalog language, and cooks for preparing the food.

Cost and Materials

Approximate cost: $50–$200

- Food for lunch
- Advertising
- Performers

Some ideas for minimizing program costs include

- Contact your local grocery stores to see if they would be willing to donate gift certificates to offset or cover the cost of food. Note: In my experience, most stores are willing to donate for community events; however, expect at least sixty to ninety days before you receive any donations. If you plan to fund a portion or your entire program with donations, plan in advance.
- It isn't always necessary to spend money on advertising to promote your program. Contacting local media (print, television, radio, and Internet) can get your program mentioned on the nightly news or in a blurb in the local paper. At the very least, most print and Internet media outlets will allow you to add your program to their calendar of events.
- Not to generalize, but Filipinos tend to be social and eager to talk about their culture and country. Try to get local Filipino residents to volunteer for your program. If you or your colleagues don't know anyone of Filipino ancestry, try contacting a local Filipino American community organization.

Bibliography

Climo, Shirley. Illus. by Francisco X. Mora. *Tuko and the Birds: A Tale from the Philippines.* New York: Henry Holt and Company, 2008.
   See description above.
Oleksy, Walter G. *The Philippines.* New York: Children's Press, 2000.
   A general introduction to the geography, people, and customs of the Philippines.
Robles, Anthony D. Illus. by Carl Angel. *Lakas and Makibaka Hotel.* Translated by Eloisa D. de Jesús. San Francisco: Children's Book Press, 2006.
   This bilingual book, written in both Tagalog and English, tells the story of a young boy who leads a protest against a landlord threatening to evict his newfound friends.

Romulo, Liana. Illus. by Joanne De León. *Filipino Children's Favorite Stories.* Hong Kong: Periplus Publishing, 2000.

A collection of stories and myths from the Philippines, some reprinted and some never published.

Sheen, Barbara. *Foods of the Philippines.* A Taste of Culture series. San Diego: KidHaven Press, 2006.

An introduction to Filipino cuisine and recipes.

Webliography

The Filipino. www.thefilipino.com.

A good resource for finding Filipino community groups in the United States.

U.S. Department of State. "Philippines." www.state.gov/r/pa/ei/bgn/2794.htm.

A current profile on the Philippines and Philippine American relations.

Vietnamese Mythology: A Middle School Odyssey

By Chadwick B. Stark

Age Level

12–14 years

Duration of Library Program

This program occurs monthly, two classes per day in the course of two days.

Overall Goal

This program aims to develop respect for Vietnamese Americans, a culturally profound civilization and ethnic group whose cultural roots reach back thousands of years.

Relevance to the Community Served

This program will help public libraries' efforts to reach out and network with their public schools, which is relevant to the communities because public libraries must strive to support initiatives in public schools for literacy and multicultural understanding.

Mythology is a great way to teach different cultures. Profiling the rich culture of Vietnam will help students to broaden their worldview, especially when most Americans most easily associate the nation with the Vietnam War.

Activities

Library Tour (20 minutes—optional)

The librarian will give a library tour and show students how to find books and how to use the computers.

Vietnamese Mythology and Fairy Tales (1 hour)

A short lecture will be presented to students, followed by group activities that include discussion and drawing.

1. Mini-lecture (10 minutes—see "Opening Mini-lecture" under "Additional Materials"). The librarian will talk about Vietnamese mythology. Ask students to pay a close attention because they will be using the information for today's lesson.

    -   Overall layout or form of Vietnamese myths—students listen and guess
    -   Why the Rooster crows at sunrise (creation myth)
    -   The story of the Owl (how/why myth)
    -   Basic mythological figures (handout—see "Important Figures")

2. Small group activity (10 minutes—see "Group Work Activities" under "Additional Materials"). Groups split into three sections and talk about their particular stories. Questions will be provided. Groups are not expected to finish all of the questions, but six are provided for groups that move quickly.
3. Small group activity wrap-up (5 minutes). Groups summarize/ share their stories with the rest of the class.
4. Introduce information about Vietnamese people and their mythology today (10 minutes—see examples in bibliography). Some information about their myths will come from www .vietnam-culture.com/zones-4-1/Myths-and-Legends.aspx.

5. Drawing fun (15 minutes). Students work in groups to create a beautiful or extremely interesting drawing of

- Something the group read about Vietnamese mythology in the story
- Something involving Vietnamese mythology that the group talked about
- A creative drawing of the countryside in Vietnam with some mythical creatures

Using glue, crayons, pens, and colored paper cutouts, groups will create a mythical Vietnamese countryside or a drawing of something from the book they read. Emphasize that the drawings should be creative and look good to present to the rest of the class.

6. Presentation (10 minutes). Each group will pick one or two group members to present their drawing. The class will discuss the some of the following:

- Was the drawing from the book?
- Was it from something we talked about today?
- What exactly is happening in the picture?
- What does this teach us about Vietnamese mythology?
- Who here today likes Vietnamese mythology and why?
- What kind of mythology do we have in the United States? How is it similar?

Preparation

Three phases must be completed to prepare for this activity at the library.

1. First phase: Getting approvals, publicity, and room reservation. Reserve rooms for the two daily class lessons over the course of two days. (It is important to obtain approval from the library's administration from very early on.) The librarian(s) in charge of the program must find, far in advance, four middle school teachers who are willing to participate in this project. This means sending out letters and e-mails, making phone calls, etc. The students will be taking a field trip during the particular day, which means that the teachers need ample time to get permission from the schools and parents. Librarians must work in advance to ensure that the teachers integrate the multicultural reading into their curricula. A promotional poster will be posted in the relevant classrooms to generate excitement.

2. Second phase: Preparing instructional materials. Students are expected to read the works in advance before coming to the public library. Photocopies must be made of several stories and sent to the teachers, because the books chosen are not available in great supply through the local OPAC. Copies made will not infringe copyright laws under Fair Use. The library can also retain the copies after the session for future use. The stories and their sources are all at equivalent reading levels:

Group 1: Livo, Norma J., and Dia Cha. *Folk Stories of the Hmong Peoples of Laos, Thailand and Vietnam.* Englewood, CO: Libraries Unlimited, 1991.
- "Gwa and Uo and Their Two Fish Wives" (9 pages)
- "Shoa and His Fire" (3 pages)
- "Pumpkin Seed and the Snake" (4 pages)
- "The Orphan Boy and His Wife" (4 pages)

Group 2: Vuong, Lynette Dyer. *The Brocaded Slipper and Other Vietnamese Tales.* New York: HarperCollins, 1982.
- "The Brocaded Slipper" (26 pages)
- "The Fairy Grotto" (17 pages)

Group 3: Vuong, Lynette Dyer. *Sky Legends of Vietnam.* New York: HarperCollins, 1993.
- "The Weaver Fairy and the Buffalo Boy" (16 pages)
- "The Seven Weavers" (22 pages)

Some of the materials should be purchased for the art project, photocopies should be made of handouts, and information literacy materials should be collated by the librarians running the information literacy/tour part of the odyssey.

3. Third phase: Promotional material production and room decoration. The rooms must be arranged for the day of the odyssey. The rooms themselves will be decorated with Vietnamese artifacts to inspire creativity and provide visual support for the project. Promotional posters will be hung around the room. A promotional poster titled "Vietnamese Mythology: A Middle School Odyssey" will be posted in the relevant classrooms by the teachers, and they will be posted in the library room on the day of the session. The promotional work will be done by the librarian in charge of the project and involves networking with the teachers, school administrators, and library administrators.

Additional promotion for the library in general will be provided by the finished products. The posters of Vietnamese mythology will be hung in the library for one month until the next project. This will be a nice display for children and parents to see the interesting programs that the library is offering.

Cost and Materials
Total cost: $50–$100

- Photocopies
- Colored pens/crayons
- Glue
- Glitter
- Colored paper
- Room décor

Bibliography

Auerbach, Susan. *Vietnamese Americans.* American Voices series. Vero Beach, FL: Rourke Publishing, 1991.
> Forced out of their country by war, Vietnamese are one group in a long line of immigrants to the shores of the United States, but with a unique set of challenges, values, and contributions.

Garland, Sherry. *Shadow of the Dragon.* San Diego: Harcourt Brace, 1993.
> Danny Vo faces the challenges of resolving conflicts between the traditional values of his Vietnamese refugee family and his adopted American culture.

Garland, Sherry. *Song of the Buffalo Boy.* San Diego: Harcourt Brace Jovanovich, 1992.
> In Vietnam, a teenage Asian American girl must flee her village to avoid a forced marriage. Reaching Ho Chi Minh City, she tries to find out about her mother and her American father.

Gilson, Jamie. Illus. by John C. Wallner. *Hello, My Name Is Scrambled Eggs.* New York: Lothrop, Lee, and Shepard, 1985.
> Young Harvey Trumble decides he's going to mold Tuan Nguyen into an American boy.

Hoyt-Goldsmith, Diane. Photos by Lawrence Migdale. *Hoang Anh: A Vietnamese-American Boy.* New York: Holiday House, 1992.
> A Vietnamese American boy living in California adapts to his new world while still holding on to his traditional customs and culture.

Huynh, Quang Nhuong. Illus. by Mai Vo-Dinh. *The Land I Lost: Adventures of a Boy in Vietnam.* New York: Harper and Row, 1982.
> The author recounts fifteen true stories of his childhood in Vietnam and village life.

Huynh, Quang Nhuong. Illus. by Jean Tseng and Mou-sien Tseng. *Water Buffalo Days: Growing Up in Vietnam*. New York: HarperCollins, 1997.

A sentimental account of a boy's childhood in the central highlands of Vietnam and his beloved water buffalo.

Livo, Norma J., and Dia Cha. *Folk Stories of the Hmong: Peoples of Laos, Thailand, and Vietnam*. Englewood, CO: Libraries Unlimited, 1991.

Twenty-seven tales of the Hmong people, from creation myths to stories of love and magic.

Vuong, Lynette Dyer. Illus. by Mai Vo-Dinh. *The Brocaded Slipper and Other Vietnamese Tales*. Reading, MA: Addison-Wesley, 1982.

These Vietnamese fairy tales echo familiar Western tales, showing that some themes are universal.

Vuong, Lynette Dyer. Illus. by Mai Vo-Dinh. *Sky Legends of Vietnam*. New York: HarperCollins, 1993.

Find out how the sun and moon got their jobs in the sky, and other tales of sky fairies in this collection of six Vietnamese tales.

Whelan, Gloria. *Goodbye, Vietnam*. New York: Knopf, 1992.

A family embarks on the risky challenges of escaping Vietnam for the freedom of Hong Kong. They must summon all of their courage and perseverance to succeed.

Webliography

Vietnam-Culture.com. "Myths and Legends." www.vietnam-culture.com/zones-4-1/Myths-and-Legends.aspx.

Excellent website explaining many aspects of this culture and its history, including myths.

Additional Materials

Opening Mini-lecture

What is a fairy tale? Fairy tales involve a story in which something *fantastic* or *unbelievable* happens. Fairy tales and folktales are told in almost every culture throughout the world, and they are usually created for children to help them understand the world. Fairy tales are not always about fairies. There is usually some great or powerful force that a person must deal with. Fairy tales can include magicians or sorceresses and they can include creatures like ogres, dragons, brownies, elves, goblins, gnomes, or leprechauns. Fairy tales involve ordinary people who have experiences of a supernatural kind and are affected by charms, disguises, spells, or other fantastic occurrences. (From the Encyclopaedia Britannica Online)

What is mythology? Mythology was mankind's first attempt to understand the world a very long time ago. Though the stories may seem fantastic or not possible, they usually represent something that actually did happen. So some parts of myths are true and others are not. Mythology exists in almost every culture of the world that has a long human history. Myths really try and answer man's questions about why we are here and why the world is the way that it is. So unlike fairy tales, myths are closer to real history. (From the Encyclopedia Britannica Online)

Vietnamese mythology and fairy tales. I have chosen to call our stories both mythology and fairy tales. Some of them refer to actual kings or royalty that lived, while others refer to people or events that are totally made up. Additionally, Vietnamese fairy tales come in different forms. Here are the forms:

> *Creation myths*—Stories that talk about how the Earth was created, or how mankind and the universe were created.
>
> *How/why myths*—Stories that explain why things are the way that they are. These are especially popular for explaining why animals and plants behave a certain way.
>
> *Stories of love and magic*—These usually involve two main people who fall in love and face evil people that try to hurt them. Magic usually saves the day.
>
> *Transformation tales*—Just like Cinderella, there are stories where people and fairies are transformed by magic into animals or other things. There is usually an evil or jealous relative who must be defeated before the main character can live happily ever after.
>
> *Fairy meddling*—This is very popular in Vietnamese fairy tales. Fairies become involved with humans when trying to help them. But they usually break the major fairy rule "Thou shalt not fall in love with a human."
>
> *Incredible events or fortune*—Many ancient Vietnamese tales describe people who are blessed by fortune. They also describe incredible feats that would not normally be possible. Often, the person who does something incredible turns out to be a fairy in disguise.

Now I'm going to read two very short stories, and I would like the class to answer these questions.

>Are they more like a fairy tales or myths? Why?
>What story forms are they? Is this story an example of
>>fairy meddling? A story of love and magic? What
>>about a creation myth? Why do we think so? Please,
>>let's support our statements with proof and ideas!

Important Figures or Themes in Vietnamese Fairy Tales and Myths

Ancestor worship: Vietnamese people worship their dead ancestors. This tradition goes far back into their history. Vietnamese myths have many examples of worshipping dead relatives.

Areca nut: An edible nut that comes from the areca palm tree and is used in ceremonies. It has special significance for Vietnamese people, and it is found in many old stories.

Betel: This is a type of vine that is combined with the areca nut and chewed, producing a bright red juice that is spicy and bitter. The combination of areca and betel is a symbol of friendship and was used for courtship in the past. Like the areca nut, betel is part of the old Vietnamese tradition that is found in many old stories.

Dragon King: The Dragon King is supposed to live under the great lakes of Vietnam—though the Hmong people say that he lives in the rivers. He is the original father of all of the Vietnamese people. The mother is the queen of the fairies. The Dragon King taught the Vietnamese people how to farm and he watched over them, saving them during hard times.

Dragons: Dragons are considered to be symbols of luck, wealth, prosperity, and royalty. They are the wisest of all creatures and bring rainfall to grow crops. According to legend, the dragon has the head of a camel, horns of a deer, eyes and scales of a fish, ears of a buffalo, the body and neck of a snake, claws of an eagle, and feet of a tiger. Dragons breathe smoke that can be turned into fire or water, and they live in the sky, on the earth, or in the sea.

Earth Spirit (Ong Dia): A fat, jolly old man who is bald. He usually has a long beard, though he is sometimes beardless. He rules each town or locality for the Jade Emperor.

Fairies (Tien): These are heavenly creatures that look like people, but they are very beautiful and they live forever. One day in their land is equal to one year in the human world. They live in the sky, in palaces along the Milky Way galaxy. The Vietnamese call the Milky Way *Ngan Ha* or the Silver River. Fairies were allowed to help humans, but not to fall in love with them.

Jade Emperor (Ngoc Hoang): The ruler of the fairies with his wife, the Queen Mother of the West (*Tay Vuong Mau*). He is a man with a black beard who wears a robe with pictures of golden dragons. His crown has thirteen jewels and his throne is carved with dragons. He is the great judge of all humans and fairies. His palace is built of the precious stone jade.

Kitchen gods: The Vietnamese have a strong belief in kitchen gods. There is one kitchen god for each household. The kitchen god oversees the household for one year and then reports the household happenings to the higher gods.

Monsoon: The monsoon is a time when heavy rains pass through Southeast Asia. The Vietnamese people have a monsoon myth that says that two men—*Son Tinh* (the Mountain Spirit) and *Thuy Tinh* (the Water Spirit)—were in love with the king's daughter. The Mountain Spirit won the daughter's hand in marriage. This made the Water Spirit angry. He raged and raged for months, causing terrible storms and flooding, until he finally gave up. This is a how/why story to explain the monsoon.

Phoenix: This is a very powerful creature in Vietnamese mythology. It represents virtue, grace, and royal women. The phoenix has a sharp beak, the neck of a snake, the back of a turtle, and the tail of a fish. It can soar through the skies, fly over the highest mountains, stand on waters of the rivers, and bathe in the sea. Its song is magical and its body represents the sky, the sun, the moon, the wind, the earth, and the planets. It is the symbol of peace and harmony.

Thunder Spirit: The Thunder Spirit is an important messenger of the Jade Emperor. His black beard often turns into dark storm clouds, and he makes thunder and lightening with a drum and an ax. He also punishes evil people.

Tortoise: The tortoise represents heaven and Earth—its shell is heaven and its belly is Earth. It represents long life and perfection. The symbol of the tortoise means, "May you be remembered for a thousand years."

Unicorn (Ly *or* Lan): This animal has the body of an antelope, the feet of a horse, and the tail of a buffalo; it also has a big horn on its head. It represents intelligence and goodness and appears only on special occasions. Unicorns are very shy animals that most people never see in their lifetimes, according to myth.

Group Work Activities

Let's think about the stories that we read. Each group has a list of questions. We will take ten minutes for each group to answer the questions. I will then ask each group to tell the class what they learned from the reading. We will give our answers to the class.

Group 1

Stories assigned: "Gwa and Uo and Their Two Fish Wives," "Shoa and His Fire," "Pumpkin Seed and the Snake," "The Orphan Boy and His Wife"

>   Are the stories that the group read more like a fairy tales or myths? Why?
>   What form of story is each story? Is the story read an example of fairy meddling? A story of love and magic? What about a creation myth? Why do we think so? List the name of each story here with the story form below it.
>   In "Gwa and Uo and Their Two Fish Wives," there is an old man by the river. What is the significance of this man's title? Check out the "Dragon King" definition on the handout.
>   Who is transformed in "Pumpkin Seed and the Snake"? What type of tale is this story, then?
>   What magical creatures exist in all four of the stories that your group can remember? Write them down here.
>   Write down some of the fantastic or impossible things that occur in the story "The Orphan Boy and His Wife."

Group 2

Stories assigned: "The Brocaded Slipper," "The Fairy Grotto"

>   Are the stories that the group read more like fairy tales or myths? Why?
>   What form of story is each story? Is the story read an example of fairy meddling? A story of love and magic? What about a creation myth? Why do we think so? List the name of each story here with the story form below it.

What law did Tu Thuc and Giang Huong break in the
story "The Fairy Grotto"? How does the story end
because they broke the law?

Can we think of a familiar fairy tale that resembles "The
Brocaded Slipper"? How is this fairy tale similar?

Write down some fantastic or impossible things that occur
in our two stories.

Is "The Brocaded Slipper" a story of love and magic? Why
or why not?

Group 3
Stories assigned: "The Weaver Fairy and the Buffalo Boy," "The Seven Weavers"

Are the stories that the group read more like a fairy tales or
myths? Why?

What form of story is each story? Is the story read an
example of fairy meddling? A story of love and
magic? What about a creation myth? Why do we
think so? List the name of each story here with the
story form below it.

What major rule of the fairies did Chuc Nu and Nguu
Lang break? How does the story end as their pun-
ishment for breaking the rules?

What impossible task is performed by Tlat-Nuong in "The
Seven Weavers"? What is so significant about the
completion of this task?

Are there any major gods or goddesses in either of our two
stories? What are they?

Are there fairies in disguise in either of the two stories? If
so, who is it? What type of story form could this be,
if a fairy is in disguise?

East Asian Harvest Festivals

By Tiffany K. Mahaffey

Age Level
13–16 years

Duration of Library Program
90 minutes

Introduction and Background
This program is to promote awareness of East Asian cultures. It will offer students a little glimpse into the traditions and customs of many East Asian countries. Ideally, this program will encourage students to one day explore the world outside of their city and country.

Overall Goal
To enable students to be able to describe the major ethnic and cultural groups in East Asia by introducing major customs and traditions. To help students in the community engage with Asia and boost their cultural awareness by

understanding and honoring attitudes, values, and behaviors unique to each person.

Relevance to the Community Served

This program will assist teens in broadening their worldview in an effort to support understanding of cultures other than their own. It will help students gain valuable insight and meaning into the rich cultural traditions of festivals held by the Chinese, Korean, and Vietnamese cultures.

Activities

Station 1: Chinese Moon Festival

History of the Moon Festival

The Chinese Harvest Moon Festival is celebrated on the fifteenth day of the eighth month of the Chinese lunar calendar in honor of the rice and wheat harvest. The moon is at its brightest at this time.

During the Chinese Moon Festival, families get together to view the full moon, a symbol of luck, harmony, and abundance. Festival participants will eat many different varieties of moon cakes with a good cup of piping hot Chinese tea. Along with the moon cakes, children have parades with lanterns and puppet shows.

The Chinese Moon Festival is also celebrated in Taiwan, Singapore, and Vietnam.

Craft Activity

Have students browse old magazines and websites for pictures of flowers, cut out the pictures, and use construction paper to make frames for them. These can be displayed or taken home.

Station 2: Chu Suk Festival in Korea

History of the Chu Suk Festival

Chu Suk is a Korean harvest celebration that is considered the Korean Thanksgiving. It is held on the fifteenth day of the eighth month of the lunar calendar. Memorial services are held, during which family members visit the tombs of their ancestors and offer them rice and fruit.

There is a special feast to show thanks for each other. The feast starts with a family gathering at which *songphyun* are served. These are special rice cakes made of rice, beans, sesame seeds, and chestnuts.

The eve of *Chu Suk* is called *Kang Kang Sue Wol Lae.* During this ceremony women make a circle and sing and dance. They wear their best *hanbok* (see note below). People also have wrestling demonstrations, archery, and folk music, and play a game called turtle tag. *Chu Suk* is the time to celebrate the family and give thanks for their blessings.

Note: The Korean *hanbok* is one of the most distinct aspects of Korean culture. The top part of the *hanbok* is called a *jeogori.* It is like a short blouse with long sleeves. Women also wear skirts called *chima.* This traditional clothing is brightly colored. The *hanbok* is often worn during national holidays and festive occasions. Various accessories such as foot gear, jewelry, and headdresses or hair pins complete the outfit.

Activity

The students will try on a *hanbok,* a pair of *beoseoun* (socks), and *komushin* (shoes) following instructions provided. Wearing *hanbok,* the students will learn traditional Korean bows for men and for women. A laptop computer will play a YouTube video to show how to perform the traditional Korean bows (www.youtube.com/watch?v=jNK_FAUAsmo).

Station 3: Trung Thu in Vietnam

History of the Trung Thu Festival

In Vietnam, *Têt-Trung-Thu* is a mid-autumn celebration that takes place on August 15. This is a family celebration, and children are the center of the holiday. It is an occasion for parents to show their love of their children. This festival is also called the Children's Festival. This holiday also celebrates the harvest moon, which is whiter and brighter at this time of year.

There is a parade to promote success in school. Parents buy their children lanterns so that they can be in the procession. Vietnamese market stalls sell all kinds of lanterns, but the most popular is the star lantern. The frame is made from bamboo and a candle is put in the center so that children can have light during the parade. Children also like to make or buy masks for this celebration. Traditional Vietnamese dances such as the unicorn dance are popular during the festivities.

Vietnamese parents tell their children fairy tales and give them moon cakes and other treats to eat. A favorite story is about a carp that wants to be a dragon. The carp works very hard and finally turns into a dragon. The moral of this story is that if children work hard in school, they can become anything they want.

Craft Activity

Have students make a mask for this holiday. They can make colorful masks from construction paper or use the papier-mâché mask cutout. The students can also choose to create a paper lantern.

Station 4: Food Table

The students will be able to taste samples of the different foods that are eaten during the different mid-autumn festivals. The different foods for sampling can include

Moon cakes

Moon cakes are a Chinese pastry traditionally eaten during the mid-autumn festival. Typical moon cakes are round or rectangular pastries, measuring about ten centimeters in diameter and four to five centimeters thick. A thick filling, usually made from lotus seed paste, is surrounded by a relatively thin crust and may contain yolks from salted duck eggs. Moon cakes are rich, heavy, and dense compared with most Western cakes and pastries. They are usually eaten in small wedges accompanied by Chinese tea.

Korean Rice Cakes

Songphyun is a special rice cake that Koreans eat at *Chu Suk,* made from rice, beans, sesame seeds, and chestnuts.

Station 5: Book Table

Fiction

Chinese Cinderella: The True Story of an Unwanted Daughter by Adeline Yen Mah (New York: Delacorte, 1999). *Chinese Cinderella* is an autobiography that describes the author's experiences growing up in China during the Second World War.

Farewell to Manzanar by Jeanne Wakatsuki Houston and James D. Houston (New York: Random House,

1973). *Farewell to Manzanar* is a memoir that
describes Wakatsuki (Jeanne) Houston's and her
family's experience being imprisoned at the Manzanar concentration camp as part of the United
States government's internment of Japanese
Americans during World War II, as well as events
concerning her family both before and after the
internment.

Seedfolks by Paul Fleischman (New York: HarperCollins,
1997). A collection of vignettes by thirteen characters describing the first year of a community garden
in a Cleveland immigrant neighborhood.

A Single Shard by Linda Sue Park (New York: Clarion
Books, 2001). This book is about Tree-ear, who is
an orphan boy living in a twelfth-century Korean
potters' village. When he accidentally breaks a pot,
he must work for the master to pay for the damage
by setting off on a difficult and dangerous journey
that will change his life forever.

Ties That Bind, Ties That Break by Lensey Namioka (New
York: Random House, 1999). This story is about
Ailin, a spirited Chinese girl who rebels and chooses
not to go through the painful process of having her
feet bound. Her entire life is changed because she
decides not to follow this ancient tradition.

When My Name Was Keoko by Linda Sue Park (New York:
Clarion Books, 2002). A chronicle of one family's
experience surviving in Japan-ruled Korea during
World War II. Told from the alternating points of
view of the two children, young Kim Sun-hee and
her older brother Tae-yul.

Nonfiction

*Holidays, Festivals, and Celebrations of the World Dictionary:
Detailing More Than 1,400 Observances from All 50
States and More Than 100 Nations,* compiled by Sue
Ellen Thompson and Barbara W. Carlson (Holmes,
PA: Omnigraphics, Inc., 1992). This is a compendi-
ous reference guide to popular, ethnic, religious,

national, and ancient holidays, festivals, celebrations, commemorations, holy days, feasts, and fasts. It is supplemented by a special section on calendar systems, tables of state and national public holidays, special indexes of chronological, cultural and ethnic, geographic, historical, religious, and sports holidays, and a general and key-word index.

Preparation

The school media center will be set up with stations. Each station will have information about the festival and a craft activity that represent the different East Asian countries with a mid-autumn festival. Note: Students can only make one craft, so they will only be able to visit one station. The other stations will have food samples and both fiction and nonfiction books for the students to peruse and eventually check out. Volunteers from the school community, including parents, will be contacted for donating time and materials, and for preparing food items. The librarian will locate books that are appropriate for checking out and arrange in stations.

Cost and Materials

Approximate cost: $0–$100

- Promotional materials
- Construction paper
- Scissors
- Ingredients for moon cakes
- Ingredients for Korean rice cakes

Bibliography

Lee, Peter H. *Anthology of Korean Literature: From Early Times to the Nineteenth Century.* UNESCO Collection of Representative Works. Honolulu: University Press of Hawaii, 1981.

Comprehensive collection of Korean literature covering poetry and prose from the last fourteen hundred years. Includes biographies, myths, love poems, bucolic tales, and tales of wonder.

Lee, Peter H. *A History of Korean Literature.* Cambridge, UK: Cambridge University Press, 2003.

This book is highly academic, but gives a thorough history of Korean literature beginning in 682 CE, when a royal Confucian academy was established in Korea and ending the discussion in the late twentieth century. Lee describes Korean literature as it developed, and the importance of the "Confucian canon" up to the sociopolitical writings of the 1960s and 1970s. He includes a section on the literature of North Korea.

Webliography

Enchanted Learning. "Chinese Lantern." www.enchantedlearning.com/ crafts/chinesenewyear/lantern/.

Contains activities and crafts for a multitude of disciplines.

Everything ESL website. www.everythingesl.net.

Contains forty content-based lesson plans for beginning through intermediate students of English as a new language. It also has thirty-one holiday and seasonal lesson plans.

The Family Culture website. "A Multicultural Thanksgiving: Vietnamese Mid- autumn Festival." www.familyculture.com.

Provides educational and cultural resources for diverse families and their service providers, with a special focus on Asian and multicultural families.

The Holiday Zone. "Celebrating Chuseok." www.theholidayzone.com/ chuseok/art.html.

Offers free holiday and seasonal educational resources for use in early childhood and elementary educational settings. Holiday and seasonal materials include learning games, whole language activities, writing prompts, songs, action rhymes, finger plays, printable worksheets, printable and interactive puzzles, coloring pages, art and craft activities, educational game ideas, and children's literature recommendations. Note the *Hanbok* coloring page.

Kinderart. "Paper Mache Masks." www.kinderart.com/multic/machemask .shtml.

Contains art lessons that teachers can use in the classroom with their students.

Additional Materials

Moon Festival Fact Sheet

- The Chinese Harvest Moon Festival, or Mid-autumn Festival, is one of the most celebrated Chinese holidays.
- The purpose of the festival is to celebrate the great rice and wheat harvest.
- The Moon Festival is celebrated in China, Taiwan, Singapore, Vietnam, and Korea.

- It is held on the fifteenth day of the eighth lunar month.
- East Asian families celebrate the end of the harvest season with a big feast. The families send each other moon cakes, which symbolize a way to show thanks and appreciation for each other.
- In Vietnam, the mid-autumn festival is called the *Têt-Trung-Thu*. The activities are often centered around children and education. Parents buy lanterns for their children so that they can participate in a candlelit lantern procession at dawn. Lanterns represent brightness, while the procession symbolizes success in school. Vietnamese markets sell a variety of lanterns, but the most popular children's lantern is the star lantern.
- In Korea, the mid-autumn festival is called the *Chu Suk. Chu suk* means a great day in the middle of August. It occurs during the harvest season. Thus, Korean families take this time to thank their ancestors for providing them with rice and fruits. The celebration starts with a family get-together at which rice cakes called *songphyun* are served. Then the family pays respect to ancestors by visiting their tombs and offering them rice and fruit. Family members wear *hanbok,* eat together, play traditional games, and at night, make wishes while watching the full moon.

The Kite Club

By Yudit Lam

Age Level

12–15 years

Duration

4 sessions of 45–60 minutes each

Introduction and Background

The history of kites has its origins in ancient China and other surrounding cultures, so kite flying goes beyond borders and has a global significance. Kite themes are found in fiction, from folktales to novels. In those cases, they are associated with freedom and pursuing one's dreams.

Overall Goal

The goals and objectives for this program include the increase in multicultural understanding through the promotion of books with kite themes; the introduction to history, functions, and different kite styles and techniques;

familiarization with literature and development of search skills; the promotion of library collections; and the ability to follow written instructions.

The program is family-oriented and will include outdoor activities; therefore, there are other collateral objectives. For example, family involvement in the learning and recreational processes of their children, development of group-team skills, sharing the love of literature within the family, and the promotion of outdoor activities in an attempt to contribute to healthy behaviors.

Relevance to the Community Served

Since kites are used globally, this theme allows the creation of bridges among cultures, which in the end will present an opportunity for mutual understanding. Through literature and hands-on activities, knowledge about other cultures and tolerance will be emphasized.

Activities

The program will occur weekly for the period of one month. Modifications can be made as determined by geographic location or other factors. In each session, a folktale or sections of a young adult book related to kites will be read, depending on the targeted age group. Subsequently, two kite-building techniques, from beginning to advanced levels, will be taught. The first meeting will serve as an introduction to kite history, functions, main structure, and the materials that will be used. Traditional kites use sticks and paper; there are new versions that are built with plastic and without sticks.

After these sessions, the best kite creations will be displayed at the library for another month, and at the end all the participants will be invited to meet at a local park to fly the kites.

Springtime is suggested for this activity, because it is the period of the year with the best weather conditions. Moreover, the American Kitefliers Association (AKA) and Kite Trade Association (KTAI) sponsor kite workshops during the National Kite Month (April), and they support these events with materials and national promotion.

Preparation

The activity will be promoted to schools and businesses in the area. There will also be posters at the branch entrance and fliers to hand out in the places mentioned above.

At the beginning of the program, participants will receive a schedule of the sessions containing the books and kite styles for each day and a handy bibliography to help them build the kites.

Cost and Materials

Approximate cost: $30

- Books from the library collection
- Kite materials (for ten to fifteen participants): tissue paper (variety of colors)—$10; wood sticks—$10 or donated by local hardware store; bamboo skewers (as a substitute of wood sticks)—$4; string—$2; other materials such as scissors, ruler, glue or tape.

Bibliography

Caldecott, Barrie. Illus. by Chris Fairclough. *Kites.* New York: Franklin Watts, 1990.
Kite designs with instructions on best materials to use for constructing efficient kites.

Dixon, Norma. Illus. by Linda Hendry. *Kites: Twelve Easy-to-Make High Fliers.* New York: Morrow Junior Books, 1996.
Step-by-step instructions for twelve easy-to-make kites. Includes diagrams, launching and safety tips, and kite decorations.

Eden, Maxwell. *Kiteworks: Explorations in Kite Building and Flying.* New York: Sterling, 1989.
History of kites and instructions for making twelve kites.

Eden, Maxwell. *The Magnificent Book of Kites: Explorations in Design, Construction, Enjoyment and Flight.* New York: Sterling, 2000.
This comprehensive guide to building kites includes over fifteen hundred illustrations, and detailed instructions on construction and flying basics.

Gray, Genevieve. Illus. by Floyd Sowell. *A Kite for Bennie.* New York: McGraw-Hill, 1972.
Bennie's African American family lives in difficult financial conditions, so to fulfill his dream, he builds a kite on his own.

Guerra, Rossella, and Giuseppe Ferlenga. *The Kite Making Handbook.* Newton Abbot, UK: David and Charles, 2004.
In addition to instructions for kite building, this book also provides a history of kite flying from ancient China to present-day international competitions.

Ha, Kuiming, and Yiqi Ha. Illus. by Xu Wang. *Chinese Artistic Kites.* San Francisco: China Books and Periodicals, 1990.
Detailed discussion and illustrations of kites of the Ha family of Beijing.

Hosseini, Khaled. *The Kite Runner.* New York: Riverhead Books, 2003.

> Human relationships, fathers and sons, and friends in Afghanistan in the final days of the monarchy and the present.

Kelly, Emery J. *Kites on the Wind: Easy-to-Make Kites That Fly without Sticks.* Minneapolis, MN: Lerner, 1991.

> Instructions for thirteen different kinds of kites that do not need sticks.

McCaughrean, Geraldine. *The Kite Rider: A Novel.* New York: HarperCollins, 2002.

> Twelve-year-old Haoyou has to protect his family and decides to join a circus acrobatic act, riding kites. This book is related to Chinese and Mongol folklore.

Michael, David. Illus. by Jim Robins. *Making Kites.* New York: Kingfisher Books, 1993.

> Learn how to make a windsock, superstunter, box kite, and two-stick kite with this introductory guide to kite building.

Morgan, Paul, and Helene Morgan. *The Ultimate Kite Book.* New York: Simon and Schuster, 1992.

> Build more than two hundred of the world's classic kites, guided by the full-color illustrations. In addition to providing a catalog of kites, the book also explains why kites are able to fly.

Park, Linda Sue. Illus. by Eung Won Park. *The Kite Fighters.* New York: Clarion Books, 2000.

> Two brothers in Korea of 1473 have special qualities: one has great skill at flying kites, while the other one has the building skills. The combination will help to tie their relationship.

Schmidt, Norman. *The Great Kite Book.* New York: Sterling, 1997.

> This book demonstrates how to build brightly colored kites inspired by animals. You can make a dragonfly kite or a butterfly kite, or a kite that looks like a barn swallow, monster, or bumblebee. Provides a chapter on wind dynamics and kite stability for the interested hobbyist.

Shyer, Marlene Fanta. *The Rainbow Kite.* Tarrytown, NY: Marshall Cavendish, 2002.

> A twelve-year-old boy tells his family story of facing the reality that his older brother Bennett is gay.

Webliography

General Information and References

American Kitefliers Association. www.aka.kite.org.

> Educates the public in the art, history, technology, and practice of building and flying kites.

National Kite Month. www.nationalkitemonth.org/history/.
> A nonprofit organization dedicated to the promotion and support of kiting helps plan kite festivals each spring.

Tetralite Kites. www.tetralite.com/links.html.
> Plans for ultralightweight, collapsible, multicell tetrahedral kites.

Kite Programs

Pratt, Barbara. "Kite Theme." www.fastq.com/~jbpratt/education/theme/ kites.html.
> Educational resources and links related to kites.

Thyssen, Anthony. "Anthony's Kite Workshop." www.cit.gu.edu.au/~anthony/ kites/.
> Personal website dedicated to kites and kite projects.

Easy-to-Make Kite

Gomber Kite Products International. "Kite Plan #1: Bumble Bee." www .gombergkites.com/nkm/plan1.html.
> Instructions for creating a bumblebee kite.

CHAPTER 3

Exploring Latino American Cultures

Honoring Mexico's Cultural Heritage

By Deborah Lambeth-Jones

Age Level

14–18 years

Duration of the Library Program

45 minutes

Overall Goal

Fostering understanding of diverse groups and recognition of the value of their cultural history is an important part of any student's education. The overarching goal of this program is to honor the culture of Mexicans and Mexican Americans, to promote understanding of the heritage of this group, and to encourage appreciation of the contributions of this ethnic group to the rich tapestry of our multicultural nation.

Specific objectives include having students listen to the music of the culture and relate the music to conditions of the cultural experience; familiarizing students with the variety of material the media center offers in multicultural areas; reinforcing students' knowledge of Mexican historical events, culture, and vocabulary; increasing student familiarity with basic research using electronic databases; and having students recognize a Mexican style of craft and complete a take-home project.

Relevance to the Community Served

As the population of Mexican Americans is growing in the United States, schools are increasingly enhancing the curriculum with materials of an ethnic flavor. This program would be appropriate for use during Hispanic Heritage Month, celebrated between September 15 and October 15 every year. Also, American students who are learning the Spanish language in classes can support their learning and awareness with literature of and information about the heritage of this group. This inclusion can give Mexican immigrant students a feeling of value in the schools.

Activities

The media center program was designed with five learning stations, incorporating a variety of activities to appeal to different learning styles. The classes will be divided into five groups of six or seven students by the classroom teacher prior to their arrival in the media center. Each group will rotate from one station to the next at eight-minute intervals. This amount of time allows for a brief introduction to format and expectations at the beginning of the program, as well as a very brief closure. Stations will include la Música, la Literatura, el Arte, la Investigación, and el Cinco Bingo.

La Música

For this activity, students will be seated at a table with a CD player and six sets of headphones. Students will listen to a CD with examples of Mexican folk music and answer questions to relate the music to cultural understanding. (See "Questions for Thought.") The songs include an example of mariachi music, "La Batalla," performed by Mariachi Vargas de Tecalitlan; "De Colores," performed by Joan Baez, a traditional folk song that has become a theme song for the United Farm Workers striving for fair treatment in the United States; and "La Bamba," performed by Richie Valens, an example of the fusion of Latin music with rock and roll in the late 1950s. The equipment needed for this station is one CD player/listening center with six headphones, a CD with the three selected songs, and the handout with questions for thought.

La Literatura

This station will include booktalks and book displays of Mexican and Mexican American fiction, as well as nonfiction materials such as history and geography books, art, poetry, and biographies. Materials needed for this station are books from the media center collection.

El Arte

At this station, students will be seated at tables with necessary materials and instructions to make el Ojo de Dios, or God's Eye, a wrapped yarn ornament traditional to the Huichol Indians of Mexico. (See instructions on p. 116.) Materials needed for this project include two three-inch craft sticks and five yards of brightly colored yarn per student. Although traditionally made with different colors of yarn tied together to create a pattern, in the interest of time and convenience, multicolored yarn will be used for this project.

La Investigación

Students will use subscription databases on media center computers for guided research. Students will be given a handout with simple questions about Cinco de Mayo based on information found on eLibrary, Facts on File, and Grolier Online. In the brief amount of time allotted to each station, in-depth research is not possible, and the purpose of this activity is to acquaint students with basic historical facts in a medium that most of them enjoy using. Equipment needed for this station is six computer workstations with Internet access and the worksheet with questions provided.

El Cinco Bingo

At the final station, students will participate in as many bingo games as time permits, using cards with terms related to Cinco de Mayo and Mexican culture. As the words are called out, students will use a colored marker to make a dot in the corner of the appropriate box on their cards. At the beginning of a new round, students will exchange markers, using a different color to mark subsequent games. Information about the terms may be provided as they are called out. Materials needed at this station are Bingo cards created using a tool on the website www.teachnology.com.

Preparation

Students will be informed of the program ahead of time with promotional fliers and a poster in their Spanish classroom. The display case in the school library will be decorated with miniature piñatas, a serape, Ojos de Dios, and Mexican flags. The school librarian will use CD players and headsets owned by the school library to prepare for the songs. Payment for and downloads of the songs to a CD will be arranged by school staff prior to the event. The school library has access to art materials through the library's budget. Handouts will be printed and distributed in advance to classrooms, and the Bingo cards will be printed from the website on the computer printer. Books owned by the school library will be located prior to the event for the literature station. These can be checked out by students at the end of the day.

Cost and Materials

Approximate cost: $0–$50

- Yarn and craft sticks
- Decorations
- CDs or songs purchased from iTunes or RealRhapsody

Bibliography

Nonfiction

Caistor, Nick. *Mexico.* New York: Dorling Kindersley, 1999.
>An illustrated guide for traveling in Mexico. Includes maps and tips on places to shop, dine, and find a room.

Canul, Rafael D. *Mexican Illegal Aliens: A Mexican American Perspective.* Mountain View, CA: Floricanto Press, 2005.
>Comprehensive and effective teaching guide about Mexican immigration into the United States from 1920s to the present.

Carew-Miller, Anna. *Mexican Art and Architecture.* Mexico, Our Southern Neighbor series. Philadelphia: Mason Crest, 2003.
>This book includes folk art, painting, sculpture, and the history of art in Mexico.

Carrasco, David, and Scott Sessions. *Daily Life of the Aztecs: People of the Sun and Earth.* Daily Life through History Series. Westport, CT: Greenwood Press, 1998.
>Day-to-day life in Aztec society, including religion, poetry, games, education, foods, and other topics.

Coronado, Rosa. *Cooking the Mexican Way: Revised and Expanded to Include New Low-Fat and Vegetarian Recipes.* Minneapolis, MN: Lerner, 2001.
>Recipes for Mexican cooking, including some of the most popular snacks and other dishes.

Kallen, Stuart A. *The Mayans.* San Diego: Lucent Books, 2001.
  Discusses the civilization and its history and influences on daily life.
  Includes possible causes for the downfall of the Mayan culture.
Lechuga, Ruth D., Chloë Sayer, and David Sievert Lavender. *Mask Arts of Mexico.*
  San Francisco: Chronicle Books, 1995.
  Includes many color pictures of the mask art in Mexico and background
  information about the history of how they were used in local festivals.
Longhena, Maria. *Ancient Mexico: The History and Culture of the Maya, Aztecs,
  and Other Pre-Columbian Peoples.* New York: Stewart, Tabori, and Chang,
  1998.
  A history of the various Mexican subcultures through the sixteenth century.
McDaniel, Jan. *The Food of Mexico.* Mexico, Our Southern Neighbor series.
  Philadelphia: Mason Crest, 2003.
  Fascinating recipe book that includes history and pertinent facts about the
  many dishes.
Oster, Patrick. *The Mexicans: A Personal Portrait of a People.* New York: William
  Morrow, 1989.
  Individuals tell their own stories about their lives in Mexico.
Parr, Ann. *Lowriders.* Race Car Legends series. Philadelphia: Chelsea House, 2006.
  Interesting legends about the lowriders of the 1940s. For fans who are inter-
  ested in creating similar vehicles.
Perl, Lila, and Victoria De Larrea. *Piñatas and Paper Flowers: Holidays of the
  Americas in English and Spanish = Piñatas y Flores de Papel: Fiestas de las
  Americás en Inglés y Español.* New York: Clarion Books, 1983.
  American and Hispanic holidays as they are celebrated in the Americas.
  Bilingual.
Reilly, Mary-Jo, and Leslie Jermyn. *Mexico.* Cultures of the World series. New
  York: Benchmark Books, 2002.
  Presents information about Mexico, in a format similar to what a gazetteer
  would include.
Warburton, Lois. *Aztec Civilization.* World History Series. San Diego: Lucent
  Books, 1995.
  Introduces Aztec civilization, its culture and history.

Biography

Kettenmann, Andrea. *Diego Rivera, 1886–1957: A Revolutionary Spirit in Modern
  Art.* Köln, Germany: Taschen Deutschland, 1997.
  Biographical examination of the life of famous Mexican muralist.
Milner, Frank. *Frida Kahlo.* London: PRC Publishing Ltd., 2001.
  Discusses the life of Frida Kahlo, the well-known Mexican artist who was the
  wife of the muralist Diego Rivera.

Paprocki, Sherry Beck. *Vicente Fox.* Major World Leaders series. Philadelphia: Chelsea House, 2003.

> Chronicles the life of Vicente Fox from childhood through becoming president of Mexico in 2000.

Scott, Kieran. *Salma Hayek.* Latinos in the Limelight series. Philadelphia: Chelsea House, 2001.

> Salma Hayek created a biographical film based on the life of Mexican painter Frida Kahlo. This book chronicles Hayek's life and career.

Soto, Gary. *A Summer Life.* New York: Dell, 1990.

> A well-known young adult author, Soto writes this story as an autobiographical essay of his life as a Chicano growing up in California.

Wepman, Dennis. *Benito Juárez.* World Leaders Past and Present series. New York: Chelsea House, 1986.

> Biographical interpretation of the life of one of Mexico's presidents who made various positive reforms to the country.

Poetry

Mora, Pat. *My Own True Name: New and Selected Poems for Young Adults, 1984–1999.* Houston, TX: Piñata Books, 2000.

> Well-known Hispanic young adult author Pat Mora presents a volume of poetry, containing over sixty poems, some with Spanish translations.

Stavans, Ilan. *Wáchale! Poetry and Prose about Growing Up Latino in America.* Chicago: Cricket Books, 2001.

> A celebration of diversity among Latinos in the format of poetry and stories. Bilingual.

Fiction

Anaya, Rudolfo A. *Bless Me, Ultima.* New York: Warner Books, 1994.

> This is the story of six-year-old Antonio, who seeks spiritual enlightenment under the watchful eye of Ultima, a healing woman, aka *curandera,* who helps him to discover himself.

Azuela, Mariano. *The Underdogs: A Novel of the Mexican Revolution.* New York: New American Library, 1963.

> The story of a young man, Demetrio Macias, who is forced to side with the rebels in the Mexican revolution in order to try to save his family.

Cisneros, Sandra. *Caramelo, or, Puro cuento: A Novel.* New York: Knopf, 2002.

> The stories of Celaya "Lala" Reyes's travels to Mexico City every summer from Chicago. The stories include her papa and not-so-favorite grandmother.

Cisneros, Sandra. *The House on Mango Street.* New York: Vintage Books, 1991.

> A young girl living in a Hispanic neighborhood in Chicago ponders the

advantages and disadvantages of her situation and evaluates her relationships with family and friends.

Farmer, Nancy. *The House of the Scorpion.* New York: Atheneum Books for Young Readers, 2002.

In this sci-fi thriller, Matt is the special clone of El Patrón, the 142-year-old leader of an illegal drug empire located between Mexico and the United States.

George, Jean Craighead. *Shark beneath the Reef.* New York: Harper and Row, 1989.

Indecisive about his aspirations of being a great fisherman or pursuing his education past the ninth grade, Tomas Torres confronts a shark in a scary underwater exploit and has new awareness of the significance of his choices.

Greene, Graham. *The Power and the Glory.* New York: Viking, 1946.

After the Mexican revolution of 1910, the last priest left attempts to reconcile his dual nature while being chased by the Communists.

Philip, Neil. Illus. by Jacqueline Mair. *Horse Hooves and Chicken Feet: Mexican Folktales.* New York: Clarion Books, 2003.

Retellings of folktales from Mexico, including colorful illustrations by Jacqueline Mair.

Jiménez, Francisco. *Breaking Through.* Boston: Houghton Mifflin, 2001.

A migrant from Mexico when he was four, Francisco, now fourteen, works in the fields of California but is trying to improve his life at the same time.

Jiménez, Francisco. *The Circuit: Stories from the Life of a Migrant Child.* Albuquerque: University of New Mexico Press, 1997.

The story of how a migrant family endures the hardships of working in labor camps and facing poverty.

Krumgold, Joseph. . . . *and Now Miguel.* New York: Crowell, 1953.

The story of the boy Miguel, a New Mexico sheep-farm worker who dreams of being elsewhere in the mountains.

Martinez, Victor. *Parrot in the Oven: Mi Vida; A Novel.* New York: HarperCollins, 1996.

Manny relates his coming-of-age experiences as a member of a poor Mexican American family in which the alcoholic father only adds to everyone's struggle.

Mikaelsen, Ben. *Sparrow Hawk Red.* New York: Hyperion Books for Children, 1993.

Thirteen-year-old Ricky plans to retaliate for his mother's murder by crossing into Mexico and stealing a plane from Mexican drug smugglers.

O'Dell, Scott. *The Feathered Serpent.* Boston: Houghton Mifflin, 1981.

This story is about Cortés and the capture of the glorious Aztec city of Tenochtitlán.

O'Dell, Scott. *The Spanish Smile.* Boston: Houghton Mifflin, 1982.

Lucinda learns the real truth about her dad's life when a visitor comes to her California island.

Rice, David. *Crazy Loco: Stories.* New York: Dial Books, 2001.

Nine short stories about Mexican American kids growing up in southern Texas.

Ryan, Pam Muñoz. *Esperanza Rising.* New York: Scholastic Press, 2000.

Esperanza and her mother are forced to work in Southern California labor camps after their escape from their previous life in Mexico of comfort and freedom. The era is just before the Great Depression.

Soto, Gary. *The Afterlife.* Orlando, FL: Harcourt, 2003.

Humorous at times, this story takes place in the dangerous streets of Fresno, where Chuy finally sees what his life could become if he faces reality head-on. He may even be in love. A touching story.

Soto, Gary. *Buried Onions.* San Diego: Harcourt Brace, 1997.

Nineteen-year-old Eddie discovers that his best friends may turn out to be his worst enemies after many of his relatives have been killed in violent street crimes. The city of Fresno is the setting, and it takes everything Eddie has to get through the day.

Soto, Gary. *Jesse.* San Diego: Harcourt Brace, 1994.

In Soto's first novel for young adults, a pair of Mexican American brothers seeks to escape a life of hard labor by attending junior college. Realistic, humorous, and poignant.

Soto, Gary. *Local News.* San Diego: Harcourt Brace Jovanovich, 1993.

Short stories with the theme of daily life of Mexican American teens in the Central Valley of California.

Soto, Gary. *Taking Sides.* San Diego: Harcourt Brace Jovanovich, 1991.

Basketball is the first love of Hispanic inner-city youth Lincoln Mendoza, age fourteen, but his loyalties are tested when he changes to a school in a white suburban neighborhood.

Steinbeck, John. *The Pearl.* New York: Penguin, 2002.

Great fortune is followed by tragedy when Kino, a poor Mexican pearl diver, believes he has found the answer to his prayers when he finds a very large and precious pearl.

Steinbeck, John. *Tortilla Flat.* New York: Penguin, 1997.

"Eat, drink, and be merry" may have been the motto of these pleasure-seeking Mexican American characters, who went to great lengths to enjoy an adventurous life. But tragedy strikes in the Monterey Peninsula. Told in episodes, it is humorous in parts.

Villaseñor, Victor. *Macho!* Houston, TX: Arte Público Press, 1991.

The heroic story of Roberto, seventeen, who crosses the border into the United States to work in the vegetable fields of California. He ends up assisting César Chávez in his valiant efforts to unionize the workers.

Additional Materials

La Música Questions

1. Mariachi is the traditional music of fiestas and weddings in Mexico. What does the title "La Batalla" mean, and how is this song relevant to Cinco de Mayo? What aspects of the song make it sound Mexican?
2. "De Colores" refers to the beauty of the colors of springtime. Why do you think this folk song was adopted as a theme song by Mexican Americans striving for fair treatment as farm workers in the 1960s?
3. "La Bamba" is another traditional song, which was transformed from folk song to groundbreaking Latin-infused rock and roll in the 1950s. What is lost and what is gained by combining two musical cultures?

La Investigación: Questions for Thought

1. What does the phrase "Cinco de Mayo" mean?
2. Why is it significant in Mexican history?
3. Cinco de Mayo is *not* Mexican Independence Day. What is the date that Mexico celebrates as its day of independence?
4. What was the name of the battle that took place on Cinco de Mayo and what year did it take place?
5. Why did the French invade Mexico?
6. Which other countries also invaded Mexico that year?
7. Who was the leader of the Mexican forces on Cinco de Mayo?
8. Who was the leader of the French forces?
9. Who was the president of Mexico at that time?
10. How did the battle on Cinco de Mayo affect the United States Civil War?

Answer Key to La Investigación Questions

1. What does the phrase "Cinco de Mayo" mean? *(May 5)*
2. Why is it significant in Mexican history? *(The battle that took place on this date was symbolic of fighting against the odds; or the Mexicans' courage in defeating a French force twice their size.)*

3. Cinco de Mayo is *not* Mexican Independence Day. What is the date that Mexico celebrates as its day of independence? *(September 15, 1810)*

4. What was the name of the battle that took place on Cinco de Mayo and what year did it take place? *(Battle of Puebla, 1862)*

5. Why did the French invade Mexico? *(to get repayment of the debt Mexico owed them—and to dispose of the Mexican constitutional government and set up a monarchy favorable to France)*

6. Which other countries also invaded Mexico that year? *(Spain and England)*

7. Who was the leader of the Mexican forces on Cinco de Mayo? *(General Ignacio Zaragosa)*

8. Who was the leader of the French forces? *(Gen. Charles Latrille Laurencez)*

9. Who was the president of Mexico at that time? *(Benito Juárez)*

10. How did the battle on Cinco de Mayo affect the United States Civil War? *(kept the French too busy fighting the Mexicans to help resupply the Confederate Army)*

El Arte

Ojo de Dios is an ancient symbol made by the Huichol Indians of Mexico.

Instructions

Begin by holding one end of the yarn with a finger on the back of the two crossed craft sticks. Wrap the yarn diagonally around the intersection of the sticks twice in each direction, to cover the center of the sticks.

Now begin weaving your first round. Wrap the yarn over and around the top stick, over and around the left stick, over and around the bottom stick, and over and around the right stick to complete one round.

Pull the yarn snug each time and push it toward the center. Always lay the yarn next to, NOT on top of the yarn already in place.

Continue going in the same direction until the craft sticks are covered. After the first few rounds, you will see the woven pattern of the "eye" beginning to form. When the craft sticks are covered, secure end of yarn and trim.

EL CINCO BINGO

Model your bingo cards after this example.

Mexico	Cinco de Mayo	Benito Juárez	Guadalupe	victory
Puebla	De Colores	Napoleon III	salsa	underdogs
música	mariachi	FREE SPACE	Zapotec	Veracruz
piñata	Ojo de Dios	Ignacio Zaragosa	Aztec	imperial monarchy
fiesta	burrito	Prince Maximillian	1862	ranchero

Cinco Bingo Call List

1862 (the year of the Cinco de Mayo battle)

Imperial monarchy (the type of government by which the French ruled Mexico)

Victory (the Mexican forces were victorious on May 5)

Mexico

Veracruz (port where the French invaded Mexico)

Zapotec (native Mexican Indians)

Cinco de Mayo (date of the battle in which a small Mexican force defeated the much larger French army)

Ojo de Dios (Eye of God, a Mexican craft)

Prince Maximillian (French ruler of Mexico from 1864 to 1867)

Burrito (a traditional Mexican food)

Salsa (a type of Mexican music, or a sauce for Mexican foods)

Ignacio Zaragosa (general who led the Mexican forces on Cinco de Mayo)

Puebla (the town where the battle of Cinco de Mayo took place)

Música (a big part of Cinco de Mayo celebrations)

Guadalupe (Mexican fort that also put up strong resistance to the French)

Underdogs (Mexican forces on Cinco de Mayo were vastly outnumbered)

Aztec (native Mexican Indians)

"De Colores" (traditional Mexican folk song)

Fiesta (a Mexican party)

Maracas (musical instrument)

Mariachi (traditional Mexican music)

Piñata (popular Latin American party decoration and game)

Benito Juárez (president of Mexico in 1858–1864)

"La Bamba" (Mexican folk song that became the first Latin-rock crossover hit)

"La Batalla" (the Battle of Puebla was the event that made Cinco de Mayo memorable)

Napoleon III (French emperor who invaded Mexico)

Ranchero

El Día de los Muertos

By Sara James and Ashley Ann Fisher

Age Level
12–16 years

Duration of Library Program
90 minutes

Introduction and Background

El Día de los Muertos (the Day of the Dead) is celebrated by people in Mexico and by Mexican Americans. This holiday is celebrated on November 2 and is preceded by All Hallows Eve on October 31, and All Saints Day on November 1. This Mexican tradition goes back thousands of years; it was originally celebrated by the Aztecs. Today, the customs of the Aztec culture have been integrated with the Christian customs of Spanish conquistadors. Preparation is a little different in each culture, but the foundations are similar and all have similar meaning of why the day is celebrated this way. This lively holiday is bright and celebratory, where relatives of loved ones prepare special dishes that the deceased ate, create altars, prepare paper crafts, decorate graves, light candles, and sing. By mixing the symbols of death with the symbols of life, Mexican Americans teach their children to honor their loved ones and embrace life.

Overall Goal

The goals and objectives of this program are to promote an appreciation and understanding of Mexican American culture. Students will recognize the unique qualities of *el Día de los Muertos* and Mexican American culture.

Students will also recognize the similarities between Halloween and *Día de los Muertos*. Students will become familiar with some of the Spanish words associated with *el Día de los Muertos*.

Relevance to the Community Served

Although students come from diverse ethnic backgrounds, most are unfamiliar with the celebration of *el Día de los Muertos*. These students are more familiar with the dominant American tradition of Halloween. Many of the students may come to the program expecting scary stories and dark themes—but all, including Mexican American students, will learn about this unique Mexican holiday that celebrates death by embracing it as a part of life.

Activities

Students will arrive and settle down for a brief introduction to *el Día de los Muertos*.

- The librarian will cover important questions and information on this holiday such as

  > When are *los Días de los Muertos* during the year? (Compare a two- or three-day celebration to when it used to be a month long.)
  > Why is celebrating *los Días de los Muertos* so important for the people of Mexico and the United States?
  > Do only Mexicans celebrate this holiday?
  > Compare how celebrations were done in the past and today.
  > What food is prepared?
  > What crafts are created for the ceremonies?
  > Where are the celebrations done?

What are altars and why are they important to this holiday? What is put on an altar? (Look at the example of an altar on display in the library.)

- As a group, students will examine the components of *el Día de los Muertos* altar and interpret the meaning of each item. Students will describe the positive, life-affirming qualities of the items (*ofrendas*). Students will observe the inclusion of loved ones that have died. Students will compare some of the items to the celebration of Halloween.
- The librarian will read aloud from the introduction to *The Horned Toad Prince* by Jackie Mims Hopkins:

> People from Mexican culture make *ofrendas* to their dead relatives as a sign of respect and love. What do you think happens to people that do not show this admiration to their family members that have passed away? According to legend, they are cursed. I have a story to read to you today about a Mexican man that was cursed and his attempt to have that curse lifted.

- The students will then eat *polvorones,* listen to Mexican folk songs, and be invited to complete a craft and/or browse through the books about *el Día de los Muertos*.
- Crafts will be displayed on tables with all supplies ready for students to grab and use after directions. Librarian will explain each table— one for *calaveras* (skeletons colored and hung for decoration) and one for *papel picado* (colorful paper banners). Students can only make one craft due to time limitations.
- Students will be invited to check out any of the books on display.

Preparation

- Make an altar: A display table featuring a traditional *Día de los Muertos* altar. Altars traditionally include symbols that represent deceased loved ones alongside symbols of life. Seasonal fruits, sweet treats, candles, flowers, and skulls are commonly included. Both a Mexican flag and an American flag in the display will provide a context for the altar within the library.

- Prepare Mexican folk songs and books: A large selection of books and music CDs about Mexico and Mexican American culture that appeal to the target audience. For example, Mariachi Autentico Mexicano. [sound recording] Los Angeles: Delta Music Inc., 1998 (www.sabob.com/products/Mariachi_Autentico_Mexicano.html).
- Make or buy *polvorones*
- Make a Spanish vocabulary sheet
- Prepare materials for crafts: Examples of the completed craft should be on display. Library assistants and/or parent volunteers should be available to provide assistance. See below for the details of the two crafts: *calaveras* (skeletons colored and hug for decoration) and *papel picado* (colorful paper banners):

> Materials for *calaveras* (paper skeletons). Prepare at least twenty to forty of each material depending on the number of participants: premade sheets of skeleton to put together after coloring; scissors, markers, colored pencils, crayons, single-hole punch; string or yarn for hanging as decoration
>
> Materials for *papel picado.* Prepare at least twenty to forty of each material, depending on the number of participants: 11-by-14-inch sheets of colored tissue paper (one for each student); scissors, string or yarn, glue

Cost and Materials

Approximate cost: $75 to serve 100 students

- Materials for crafts
- Food: *polvorones*

Bibliography

Ancona, George. *Pablo Remembers: The Fiesta of the Day of the Dead.* New York: Lothrop, Lee, and Shepard, 1993.
This thoroughly descriptive informational book chronicles a Mexican family during three days of celebration. Beginning on All Hallows Eve and concluding at the end of the Day of the Dead, readers follow the family through simple text and beautiful color photographs. Important Spanish words are repeated and translated throughout.

Chambers, Catherine. *All Saints, All Souls, and Halloween.* A World of Holidays series. Austin, TX: Raintree Steck-Vaughn, 1997.

This general overview explores three related holidays and how people have celebrated them in different countries throughout history.

England, Tamara. Illus. by Geri Strigenz Bourget. Photographs by Mark Salisbury and Jamie Young. *Josefina's Craft Book: A Look at Crafts from the Past with Projects You Can Make Today.* Middleton, WI: Pleasant Company, 1998.

This book contains instructions, diagraphs, and photographs of authentic Mexican crafts.

Garza, Carmen Lomas, Harriet Rohmer, and David Schecter. *Magic Windows.* San Francisco: Children's Book Press, 1999.

This beautiful picture book is based on Carmen Lomas Garza's cut-paper art. The narrative is written in Spanish and English, and each page describes the story behind the visual art. The images focus on family life, indigenous animals, and folklore.

Greenleigh, John, and Rosalind Rosoff Beimler. *The Days of the Dead: Mexico's Festival of Communion with the Departed.* San Francisco: Collins Publishers San Francisco, 1991.

Photographer John Greenleigh provides excellent illustrations of *los Días de los Muertos* based on his travels to small Mexican towns. His photo documentary of the festival is accompanied by text written by cultural scholar Rosalind Rosoff Beimler.

Hopkins, Jackie Mims. Illus. by Michael Austin. *The Horned Toad Prince.* Atlanta, GA: Peachtree, 2000.

This hilarious fractured version of "The Frog Prince" is set in the American southwest. Written in the dialect of Texas ranchers and Spanish-speaking Mexican Americans, this tale makes for a great read-aloud.

Morrison, John. *Frida Kahlo.* The Great Hispanic Heritage series. Philadelphia: Chelsea House, 2003.

This biography of Frida Kahlo is geared to teen readers. The pain and joy of this talented painter's life is chronicled in this well-organized biography, which is illustrated with Kahlo's paintings. Well-defined chapters and subheadings guide teen readers through the informational text.

Webliography

Minnesota Historical Society. "Day of the Dead Library Display." www.mnhs .org/library/dayofdead/html/librarydisplay.html.

Information and photos about the Minnesota Historical Society's Day of the Dead library display.

Pan de Muertos recipe, www.mexconnect.com/mex_/recipes/puebla/ kgpandemuertos.html.

Additional Materials

Sample promotional e-mail to teachers

Dear Teachers,

You are all invited to sign your classes up for a *Día de los Muertos* celebration in the library. This forty-five-minute program will be held in the [insert library name] Library on [insert date]. Students will be introduced to the celebration of *el Día de los Muertos* and will learn about the symbols that make up this joyous holiday. The celebration will include treats, music, a craft, and the opportunity to check out a book. Check your mailbox for a promotional flier to post in your classroom.

Hispanic Heritage Month
By Nicolette Dewsbury

Age Level
12–18 years (can be a family event)

Duration of Library Program
4 weeks; library patrons can drop in as they like

Overall Goal
The goal is to enhance communication between Hispanic and non-Hispanic communities, educate nontraditional library users about library services available to them, and further the library's overall goal of becoming a center of the community.

Relevance to the Community Served
This program will help both Hispanics and non-Hispanic groups celebrate the Hispanic culture throughout Hispanic Heritage Month (September 15 to October 15). This is relevant because it will enhance the knowledge of Hispanic teens of their own cultural heritage celebrations as well as teach American students about the culture of their Hispanic classmates.

Activities

The program will be divided into four weeklong segments honoring different countries where Hispanics originally came from.

First Week: Mexico

The first week will honor Mexico, beginning with a kickoff on September 15 celebrating Mexican Independence Day. On the closest Saturday to September 15, there will be a street fair outside of the library. Musicians, storytellers, and dancers will be featured prominently on a center stage. Around the stage will be multiple vendors offering Hispanic wares, including a variety of food and clothing.

Inside, the library will be decorated with Mexican flags and pictures representative of Mexico culture, along with balloons in red, white, and green. A display of books for young adults will be featured, including such books as Pam Ryan's *Esperanza Rising*.

Second Week: Central America

The second week will honor the remaining countries of Central America (excluding Mexico) and the Caribbean Islands of Hispanic origin. In addition to booktalks given by library personnel, an hour can be used for a storytelling of the book *The Song of El Coqui and Other Tales of Puerto Rico* by Nicholasa Mohr for younger kids. There will be a variety of flags representing the different countries available for coloring, and a map of the Caribbean and Central America for older children to fill in.

Third Week: South America

This week will honor the cultures of South America. The event for teens and older adults or parents will be a storytelling of the book *One Hundred Years of Solitude,* by Gabriel García Márquez. An added story hour will be designed around older children (third through sixth grades) that features *On the Wings of the Condor* by Alma Flor Ada, which highlights the history and culture of Latin America. There will be an additional storytelling hour for preschoolers thru second grade that would use *¡Pío Peep!,* a bilingual book by Alma Flor Ada and F. Isabel Campoy featuring Latin American nursery rhymes.

Again, a variety of flags will be available for coloring, along with a handout explaining what each color on the individual flags represents. A handout will be available for older children allowing them to color and fill in a map of South America.

Fourth Week: Spain

Week four will revolve around Spain. A translation of the book *Don Quixote* by Cervantes will be included in some booktalks for teens and adults. For the older children thru teenagers, there will be scavenger hunts varying in age appropriateness with questions about Spain, its history, culture, food, and holidays. A storytelling hour for preschoolers through second grade can take place simultaneously and will feature *The Beautiful Butterfly: A Folktale from Spain,* by Judy Sierra. A flag handout will be available for coloring along with questions about the flag and its meaning.

Activities Spanning All Four Weeks

The library displays highlighting the various countries will be rotated on a weekly basis, featuring new books and handouts every week. When children complete a handout, there will be a small prize such as a piece of candy. (See "Famous Hispanics" in "Additional Resources.") Every Saturday during Hispanic Heritage Month will feature library tours of the Spanish collection and the library's Spanish web portal for the older children and their families, in hopes of getting them involved in the library. An effort would also be made to recruit authors of Hispanic heritage to conduct author/writing workshops and booktalks and storytelling sessions on several of the four Saturdays.

Preparation

The month previous to the start of the Hispanic segment will entail posters and fliers advertising upcoming activities. Every library patron will receive a flier upon checkout, and there will be a stack placed for disbursement near the entrance/exit of the library. These fliers and posters will be in both Spanish and English in order to be effective in reaching the desired segments of the population.

The library should also check into placing an ad in the local Spanish newspaper in an effort to promote the event. Grant funding can be researched in order to help offset the cost of the program and enable the library to enrich the program to new heights. Contact local Hispanic social services agencies in the hopes of forming a partnership to provide services and resources beyond the scope of the library and to receive education from the agency about ways to reach out to the Hispanic population.

The library should make sure to have a wide variety of Hispanic materials and literature, requesting loans from cooperative libraries if necessary to ensure a rich and varied collection.

Cost and Materials

Approximate cost: $100

- Permit for street fair
- Craft materials and handouts
- Promotional fliers and posters
- Selected literature will be procured from the library's collection
- Mexican flag(s), balloons, and other decorations
- Food and fair items can be covered under donations and cooperative developments with local Hispanic business and social clubs.

Bibliography

Ada, Alma Flor, and F. Isabel Campoy. Illus. by Felipe Dávalos, Bruno González, and Claudia de Teresa. *On the Wings of the Condor.* Gateways to the Sun series. Miami, FL: Alfaguara Young Readers, 2004.
A beautifully illustrated novel about the history and culture of Spanish-speaking lands.

Ada, Alma Flor, and F. Isabel Campoy. Adapted by Alice Schertle. Illus. by Viví Escrivá. *¡Pío peep! Traditional Spanish Nursery Rhymes.* New York: Harper-Collins, 2003.
An excellent collection of twenty-nine nursery rhymes from Spain and Latin America. In Spanish, with English translations.

Alvarez, Julia. *Before We Were Free.* New York: Knopf, 2002.
Author Julia Alvarez tells a story about the adolescence, perseverance, and struggle of Anita de la Torre, a twelve-year-old girl who fled the Dominican Republic with her family, looking for freedom.

Alvarez, Julia. *How the García Girls Lost Their Accents.* Chapel Hill, NC: Algonquin Books of Chapel Hill, 1991.
Told from their adulthood backward, this book reviews America's effect on four sisters who fled the Dominican Republic in childhood.

Anaya, Rudolfo A. *Bless Me, Ultima.* New York: Warner Books, 1994.
An award-winning story of a young boy set in New Mexico in the 1940s. When Ultima, a *curandera* (a traditional folk healer who cures people with herbs and shamanic magic), comes into his life, Antonio gradually opens his eyes to his bonds with his culture and stories of the past.

Canales, Viola. *The Tequila Worm.* New York: Wendy Lamb Books, 2005.
A story of a girl growing up in a close-knit community of the barrio in McAllen, Texas, a place full of the magic and mystery of family traditions. She wants to explore life beyond the barrio as she has experiences as a scholarship student at an Episcopal boarding school in Austin, but instead discovers her strong bond to family and tradition. Pura Belpré Award winner.

Cofer, Judith Ortiz. *An Island Like You: Stories of the Barrio.* New York: Orchard Books, 1995.
> Twelve short stories about adolescents attempting to fit in at home, school, and work while coming to terms with their Puerto Rican heritage.

Hoyt-Goldsmith, Diane. Illus. by Lawrence Migdale. *Day of the Dead: A Mexican-American Celebration.* New York: Holiday House, 1994.
> Ten-year-old twins from Sacramento, California, tell the story of their family's Day of the Dead celebration, focusing on celebrations of an American family living in a Mexican American community. It explains Aztec beliefs and their intermingling with Catholic rituals, dancing, art, and prayer that illustrate the unity of past and present during festival days.

Jiménez, Francisco. *The Circuit: Stories from the Life of a Migrant Child.* Audio-cassette or CD-ROM. Northport, ME: Audio Bookshelf, 2001.
> A collection of autobiographical stories of an illegal migrant worker's son who was born in Mexico, spent his childhood alternating between migrant farm work and the classroom, and later became an established professor at Santa Clara University, California.

Márquez, Gabriel García. *One Hundred Years of Solitude.* New York: Harper and Row, 1970.
> A novel portraying one hundred years in the mythical town of Macondo, through the lives of its founder and his descendants.

Mohr, Nicholasa, and Antonio Martorell. *The Song of el Coquí and Other Tales of Puerto Rico.* New York: Viking, 1995.
> A collection of three folktales about three animals, each describing one of the three dominant cultures of Puerto Rico: the Taínos, the Africans, and the Spaniards.

Ryan, Pam Muñoz. *Esperanza Rising.* New York: Scholastic Press, 2000.
> Thirteen-year-old Esperanza faces a dramatic change in her life after the death of her father. She goes from a wealthy family in Mexico to facing the harsh life of a migrant farm worker in California. Based on the true life of the author's grandmother.

Sierra, Judy. Illus. by Victoria Chess. *The Beautiful Butterfly: A Folktale from Spain.* New York: Clarion Books, 2000.
> A melding of two classic folktales about a butterfly's love for a sweet mouse.

Soto, Gary. *Buried Onions.* San Diego: Harcourt Brace, 1997.
> A story of a junior college dropout. Nineteen-year-old Eddie struggles to find a place for himself as a Mexican American living in a violence-infested neighborhood of Fresno, California.

Soto, Gary. *A Fire in My Hands: A Book of Poems.* New York: Scholastic, 1990.
> Twenty-one poems about the themes of life, each presented with a personal anecdote.

Villaseñor, Victor. *Burro Genius: A Memoir.* New York: Rayo, 2004.

> A memoir of renowned writer Victor Villaseñor, author of *Rain of Gold.* Highly gifted and imaginative as a child, the writer tells his story of coping with an untreated learning disability and the frustrations as a Latino boy in an English-only American school in the 1940s.

Villaseñor, Victor. *Macho!* Houston, TX: Arte Público Press, 1991.

> This novel tells a story of seventeen-year-old Roberto Garcia's experience as an illegal Mexican immigrant laborer whose American dream faces brutal reality.

Webliography

Enchanted Learning. www.enchantedlearning.com/Home.html.

> A website that offers a wide variety of worksheets, along with crafts divided by culture and activity suggestions.

Additional Materials

Name _____   Teacher _____

Directions: Use classroom, library, and Internet resources to learn about the ten famous Hispanics and Latinos listed below. On the line next to each name, write the letter of the statement that describes that person.

FAMOUS HISPANICS

Person/People	Why Famous?
1. Ellen Ochoa _____	A. discovered the Mississippi River
2. Juan Ponce de León _____	B. a world-famous musician who played the cello
3. Hernando de Soto _____	C. led fight for a better life for migrant farm workers
4. Father Junipero Serra _____	D. a Cuban physician who discovered that yellow fever was spread by a bite from a mosquito
5. Sonia Sotomayor _____	E. discovered Florida
6. Pablo Casals _____	F. baseball player with Pittsburgh Pirates from 1955–1972
7. Frida Kahlo _____	G. influential Mexican artist known for self-portraits
8. Carlos Juan Finlay _____	H. first Hispanic woman appointed to the U.S. Supreme Court
9. Cesar Chavez _____	I. first Hispanic woman in space
10. Roberto Clemente _____	J. founder of the California missions

Key: 1—I; 2—E; 3—A; 4—J; 5—H; 6—B; 7—G; 8—D; 9—C; 10—F

Time for Cuba

By Louise Gestwicki

Age Level

12–18 years

Duration of Library Program

60–75 minutes

Introduction and Background

As with members of many cultures in the United States, young Cuban Americans often shed their cultural identity to assimilate and "Americanize." This program will be of interest to these young adults, leading them to read books and poetry by Cubans or check out a biography of a famous Cuban American. Ideally the program will create interest for young adults to ask friends and family about their experiences in Cuba or growing up as a Cuban American.

Overall Goal

The goal of the program is to present the audience with Cuban literature, music, dances, and foods in order to successfully get young adults interested in the rich culture of the Caribbean country. Another goal is to present a program about Cuba lasting from an hour to an hour and a half that will be of interest to an audience between the ages of twelve and eighteen.

Patrons who have recently arrived from other countries are often amazed that the library is a free service. Offering such a program will draw these patrons into the library and provide library staff with the opportunity to raise awareness about the library's free services to this population. By offering a cultural event that Cuban and Cuban American teens can relate to, the program will also attract young people who may frequent the library, but do not normally participate in library events. Parties and family gatherings often include music and dancing, so the demonstration should pique young people's interest.

Relevance to the Community

Cubans have been immigrating to the United States since the late 1950s; many young patrons have grandparents, parents, or friends who grew up in Cuba. Young adults may assimilate quickly and forget their roots. This program hopes to capture (or recapture) their interest in these Afro-Caribbean roots. The United States is home to many successful politicians and pop-culture icons of Cuban descent. The program will celebrate Cuban and Cuban Americans who can serve as role models for young adults.

This program will also be relevant to other teens, who often have friends of Cuban heritage and may have great interest in their historical background.

Activities

An attractive display can be created prior to the event. Some books that could be included are *Dreaming in Cuban,* by Cristina García; *Alicia Alonso: First Lady of Ballet,* by Sandra Arnold; and *Versos Sencillos/Simple Verses,* by José Martí. If a bilingual librarian or volunteer is available, she can spend about fifteen minutes reading selections in English and Spanish from a book such as *Cuentos para Chicos y Grandes* and read selected poems in both languages from *Versos Sencillos/Simple Verses* (poems VI and XXXIX).

After reading passages from these books, the librarian can present a fifteen-minute booktalk on works such as *Flight to Freedom,* by Ana Veciana-Suarez. Audience members should be encouraged to tell personal stories about hardships they or their family endured as Cubans or Cuban Americans, or as immigrants from any other country.

Traditional Cuban finger foods, *pastelitos* and *bocaditos,* can be served while Cuban music is played. As the refreshments are passed, play music by Celia Cruz, the "Queen of Salsa," and the dancers can come out and begin their performance. The dancers can perform different dances that are popular in Cuba or that originated there. *Rueda de Casino* is a popular group-style dance that started in Cuba during the 1960s, and salsa is a dance with partners. The dancers can perform simple demonstrations in which the audience can participate. This portion should last about thirty minutes; but can last longer if the audience is enthusiastic about participating.

Preparation

This program can be planned to coincide with Hispanic Heritage Month (September 15 through October 15), with the birthday of a popular Cuban figure such as Celia Cruz (October 21) or José Martí (January 28), or with a significant event in Cuban culture.

The librarian may try to find a Spanish-speaking librarian or volunteer who is willing to read or translate some of the selections for the program, visit local dance studios or community centers to see if a group is willing to dance for the program for free, and visit local bakeries to see if one is willing to donate *pastelitos* and *bocaditos.*

Fliers created for the event may be handed out during outreach at nearby schools, community centers, and other relevant locations.

To promote the event within the library, prepare a display with materials about different aspects of Cuban culture, that is, literature, books on Cuban cuisine and history, DVDs about salsa dancing, and pictures of Cuban celebrities. Some famous Cubans and Cuban Americans that can be included are musicians such as Celia Cruz, Gloria Estefan, Pit Bull, Christina Milian, and Jon Secada. Some Cuban and Cuban American celebrities are Cameron Diaz, José Canseco, Livan Hernandez, and historical figures such as José Martí.

Cost and Materials

Approximate cost: $0–$25

- Food (*bocaditos* and *pastelitos*). Solicit local bakeries to donate refreshments for the program
- Decorations (optional)

Bibliography

Ada, Alma Flor. *Under the Royal Palms: A Childhood in Cuba.* New York: Atheneum Books for Young Readers, 1998.

> A series of short stories about the author's life growing up in Cuba. The author describes how some families grow up with nothing while others have anything they need or want. This historically accurate book makes a great addition for the younger audience that attends the program, but the book would be enjoyed by all.

Ada, Alma Flor. Illus. by Antonio Martorell. *Where the Flame Trees Bloom.* New York: Atheneum Books for Young Readers, 1994.

> A collection of eleven stories about the author's childhood in Cuba. Each of the stories is unique and told by different family members. The stories in the book exemplify strong family values. This book is appropriate for eight- through twelve-year-olds.

Arnold, Sandra Martín. *Alicia Alonso: First Lady of the Ballet.* New York: Walker, 1993.

> Alicia grew up in Cuba and became one of the primary ballerinas during the early years of the American Ballet Theatre. She nearly went blind in her early twenties, and finally succeeded in forming her own ballet company in Cuba. The book is historically accurate and gets the reader interested in learning about the Revolution era in Cuba. This title is recommended for young adults.

García, Cristina. *Dreaming in Cuban.* New York: Knopf, 1992.

> This book shows the trials and tribulations dealt with by women in a Cuban family. Each generation goes through difficult times dealing with the Revolution. Celia, the eldest del Pino, lives in Cuba, and has blind faith and support for Fidel Castro. Her son has moved to Czechoslovakia and her daughter Felicia suffers from mental problems and practices Santería to heal herself. Another character, Lourdes, lives in Brooklyn after she fled Cuba, and has immersed herself in American culture. The story is recommended for older teens and adults.

Lamazares, Ivonne. *The Sugar Island.* Boston: Houghton Mifflin, 2000.

> This novel is set in Cuba during the late 1960s and early 1970s. Tanya's mother runs off to join the revolution when Tanya is young, leaving her to be brought up by her grandmother. When Mama returns she plans an escape to Miami for a better life. The plan fails and she gets sent to prison. Historically accurate descriptions in this book make it ideal for the program, because it offers a different viewpoint by showing two different sides of life in Cuba and in the United States. This book is recommended for older teens and adults.

Martí, José, and Manuel A. Tellechea. *Versos Sencillos = Simple Verses.* Houston, TX: Arte Público Press, 1997.

A collection of poems written by notable nineteenth-century Cuban writer and revolutionary José Martí. The book has an English translation provided alongside the Spanish version of each poem. This title is recommended for those not familiar with Martí's works and for adults and older teens interested in poetry.

Perera, Hilda. Illus. by Rapi Diego. *Cuentos para Chicos y Grandes.* New York: Scholastic/Lectorum Publications, 2001.

A series of short stories written in Spanish by renowned Cuban author Hilda Perera. If a librarian or volunteer is bilingual, having her read one of the *cuentos* in Spanglish (English and Spanish mixed) would be a great asset to the program.

Perera, Hilda. Illus. by Mathieu Nuygen. *Kiki: A Cuban Boy's Adventures in America.* Coconut Grove, FL: Pickering Press, 1992.

Kiki's parents send him to live in Miami when he is eight years old in order to escape Cuba's communism. Kiki's "firsts" are comically integrated into the story of his new life in South Florida as he lives in different neighborhoods, rich and poor. Young immigrants or children of immigrants can relate to this story. This book is geared toward a younger audience (age nine through thirteen) but anyone would enjoy it.

Veciana-Suarez, Ana. *Flight to Freedom.* First Person Fiction series. New York: Orchard Books, 2002.

Told through the journal of thirteen-year-old Yara Garcia, this book depicts the difficulties faced by young people when they move from Cuba to the United States. Yara writes about communism in Cuba, and then her struggle to assimilate once she moves to Miami. This book is recommended for middle school students.

Puerto Rican Heritage Program for *Día de la Abolición de Esclavitud* (Day of the Abolition of Slavery, March 22)

By Ryan P. Gray

Age Level
12–18 years

Duration of Library Program
1 day

Introduction and Background
This inclusion program can be understood through its cross-curricular objectives:

Geography: Students will study the location of Puerto Rico, its topography, climate, and its latitude and longitude. Students will also study the wildlife of Puerto Rico.

Language arts: Earlier in the week, students will read a section from the book *Growing Up Puerto Rican*. Class discussion will include comparisons between the experience they read about and their own life experience growing up. During the fiesta, Puerto Rican poetry will be read in both Spanish and English by the high school or middle school Spanish classes.

Social studies: This event will be integrated into the high school or middle school social studies classroom. Topics discussed in social studies will include the relationship between the government of Puerto Rico and the United States government. The concept of "citizen" will be discussed, including why residents of Puerto Rico are citizens of the United States, even though they have no voting representative or senator in congress and cannot vote for president.

History: Because March 22 is the day that slavery was abolished in Puerto Rico, the history of the slave trade in Puerto Rico and in the Americas more generally will be covered. Other topics of Puerto Rican history will also be discussed.

Art: The high school or middle school art class will be able to integrate this event into lesson plans, and at the same time help keep down the overall cost of the event by having students draw or paint images from Puerto Rico or draw Puerto Rican–style art. These finished works of art can help decorate the school media center, school hallways, and other involved parts of the school.

Music: The choir and the band will learn to perform traditional Puerto Rican music in weeks leading up to this event.

Science: The science class will study the climate and weather patterns of Puerto Rico and the area of the Caribbean in which it is situated. Special emphasis will be placed on the impact the wind patterns have on the prevalence of hurricanes in the region. The flora and fauna of the island will also be studied.

Overall Goal

The overall goal of this program is to educate the target audience about the culture of the people of Puerto Rico and the people of Puerto Rican heritage elsewhere in the United States. An effort will be made to cover the roots of Puerto Rican culture, including Taíno, Spanish, African, and mainland United States and the contributions of this culture to the fabric of American society both within the Commonwealth of Puerto Rico and the United States mainland.

Relevance to Community Served

Many Americans do not know about the history of the Commonwealth of Puerto Rico, which the United States acquired as a result of the Spanish American War. This program is relevant to families and children in educating them about the commonwealth, featuring the Day of the Abolition of Slavery, which occurs on March 22 every year.

Activities

After the cross-curricular activities described above are delivered in the classroom, the media center will throw a Puerto Rican fiesta in celebration of *Día de la Abolición de Esclavitud*. This event will include traditional Puerto Rican music, food, contests, and a reading of Puerto Rican poetry in both Spanish and English by members of the high school Spanish class. The TAG will select music, poetry, and prizes that are to be used for the event.

Music sung by Grammy Award winner and Puerto Rican Ricky Martin (such as "Living La Vida Loca") will play in the background during the event. Students will read poems by one of the leading twentieth-century poets, Evaristo Ribera Chevremont.

Parents will be asked to donate finger foods, such as *surullitos* (sweet plump cornmeal fingers) and *empanadillas* (crescent-shaped turnovers filled with various ingredients).

For contests, library staff will come up with written questions and answers about Puerto Rico and its history, which may have been covered in the previous curricular activities. Depending on the number of participants, there may be two large teams or four to six teams that can play tournament games, and the winning team will receive prizes. Use numbers drawn at the door to designate teams as students arrive.

Preparation

In advance of the event, consultation and coordination will be made with teachers and administrators. Instructors whose classes are likely to have a special interest in this event (e.g., Spanish and art) will be consulted on specific aspects that are in their areas of expertise.

Flyers will be created announcing the fiesta and the research contest.

The school library itself will be decorated in a Puerto Rican fiesta theme. Many of these decorations can be produced in-house by high school or middle school art classes. Some decorations, such as colorful streamers, may need to be purchased.

Cost and Materials

Approximate cost: $0–$100

Some books may need to be purchased in preparation for this event, but once this event is over, these materials will become part of the general collection. The cost of these books can therefore be absorbed by the general media center book budget.

Much of the cost of food will be absorbed by participating parents, who will bring in traditional Puerto Rican foods. The remaining costs mostly involve decorations, party favors, and prizes for the contest.

Bibliography

Cofer, Judith Ortiz. *The Meaning of Consuelo.* New York: Farrar, Straus, and Giroux, 2003.
> A young girl tells her tragic story of coming of age in 1950s Puerto Rico. Consuelo struggles to understand her place in the world as her father embraces each technological advance and the promise of wealth it offers, her mother reaches for the past and the natural beauty of the island, her closest friend and cousin begins to reveal his homosexuality, and her younger sister slips quietly into madness.

De Jesús, Joy, ed. *Growing Up Puerto Rican: An Anthology.* New York: William Morrow, 1997.
> A fine ethnic anthology of Puerto Ricans, published in the same series as *Growing Up Asian American* (1993) and *Growing Up Native American* (1993). A series of short stories, memoirs, and essays present rich and various aspects of Puerto Rican childhood and young adulthood, both in the United States and on the island. Contributing authors include both established and new authors. This book gives an insider's look at what it is like to be a Puerto Rican.

Chevremont, Evaristo Ribera. *Antología Poética, 1924–1950.* San Juan: Universidad de Puerto Rico, 1957.
> One of the leading twentieth-century poets who wrote about both urban and rural life. This poetry collection includes his poems composed between 1924 and 1950.

Santiago, Esmeralda, *Almost a Woman.* Reading, MA: Perseus Books, 1998.
> This book is a sequel to author and actress Esmeralda Santiago's childhood story, *When I Was a Puerto Rican.* It is an inspiring tale that recalls her life journey as an adolescent and young Puerto Rican woman living Brooklyn, New York, with her mother and ten siblings during the 1960s. This book provides a unique window into a Puerto Rican immigrant family that suffered through periods of poverty while exploring the new culture and opportunities available to them.

Webliography

Gonzalez-Espada, Wilson J., and Oliver, J. Steve. "Making Puerto Rican High School Physics Contextual and Culturally Relevant: A Statistical Analysis of Influencing Factors." www.eric.ed.gov/ERICDocs/data/ericdocs2sql/content_storage_01/0000019b/80/1a/1e/ee.pdf.
This resource provides a great deal of information about Puerto Rican culture from the perspective of an educator. This information can be used to assist non–Puerto Rican teachers in helping non–Puerto Rican students better understand Puerto Rican society.

Yale–New Haven Teachers Institute. "Puerto Rico . . . Its Land, History, Culture, and Literature." www.yale.edu/ynhti/curriculum/units/1987/1/87.01.04.x.html.
This is an excellent resource for teachers to find quality lesson plans for teaching about Puerto Rico.

Welcome to Puerto Rico. http://welcome.topuertorico.org/index.shtml.
This is a great web resource presenting everything about Puerto Rico, including people, geography, history, economy, government, culture, and recipes.

CHAPTER 4

Exploring Native American Cultures

National American Indian and Alaska Native Heritage Month

By Ashley Johnson and Peggy Border

Age Level

12–18 years

Duration of Library Program

1 to 5½ hours

Introduction and Background

November is National American Indian and Alaska Native Heritage Month. To honor the indigenous people of the United States, the program will include stories, crafts, food, and music. The attendees will leave with an appreciation and understanding for the culture. They will also be provided with access for further exploration of the culture through books, CDs, DVDs, and websites.

Overall Goal

The intention of this program is to provide an opportunity for the community to participate in and experience historically traditional customs and practices of Native Americans.

Relevance to the Community Served

American Indian heritage is relevant to the history of the United States, therefore this program would be beneficial to all communities and library patrons. The festivities and planned events allow for collaboration from staff, volunteers, Friends of the Library organizations, and patrons to unite in a celebration of diversity, history, and culture.

Activities

Select one or more activities:

Part 1: Stories

From 11 a.m. to noon, the young adult librarian will engage in booktalks of the following:

Alexie, Sherman. Illus. by Ellen Forney. *The Absolutely True Diary of a Part-Time Indian.* **New York: Little, Brown, 2007.**
> Touching and funny story of Junior, a young boy who transfers to an all-white school and struggles with his present and future.

Bruchac, Joseph. *Skeleton Man.* **New York: HarperCollins, 2001.**
> Exciting mystery wherein a young girl named Molly has strange dreams about her mysterious uncle and missing parents.

Part 2: Crafts

The next portion of our celebration of Native American cultures includes various craft projects. From noon to 2 p.m., attendees will be encouraged to make dream catchers or straw bookmarks. There will be an assortment of projects available for all. The projects will be set up in stations, and after the first hour, students will switch, so if people choose to stay for the full two hours, they will have access to different crafts.

Make a Dream Catcher

Crafts are made from individually packaged kits from Oriental Trading Co. These can be customized by purchasing key chain rings, ribbon, feathers, string, plastic beads, and glue.

Straw Weaving (bookmarks)

Monaghan, K., and J. Hermon. *You Can Weave! Projects for Young Weavers.* Worcester, MA: Davis Publications, Inc., 2000.

Part 3: Food

Following the craft portion of the event, offer small samples of various Native American dishes. Food can be fixed in advance and the recipes can be sent home on fliers. The following recipes will be included in the festivities.

Apache Bread

> 1 cup white cornmeal
> ½ tsp red pepper
> 1 cup yellow cornmeal
> 1 cup boiling water
> 1 tsp. salt
> ½ cup bacon drippings
> green cornhusks

Mix dry ingredients; add boiling water and bacon drippings. Form into small rolls and wrap in green cornhusks. Bake at 350 degrees for 1 hour. Makes 12 individual breads.

Pumpkin Candy

> 1 5-lb. pumpkin
> 5 cups sugar
> 1 tbsp. baking soda
> Water

Peel and seed pumpkin. Cut pumpkin into 2-by-4-inch strips. Stir baking soda into enough water to cover strips and let stand for 12 hours, then drain and wash strips in running water. Drop pumpkin into pot of boiling water, and cook until tender. Remove and crisp in ice water; drain. Mix sugar with 1 cup water and boil 10 minutes. Add pumpkin and simmer in covered pot until syrup is thick and strips are brittle. Spread strips to dry. May be stored when cold.

Pumpkin Pine Nut Bread

2 cups flour
3 eggs, beaten
1 tsp. baking soda
¾ cup milk
½ tsp. salt
½ cup oil
1½ cup sugar
1 tsp. vanilla
2 cups cooked pumpkin
1½ cups pine nuts, toasted

Heat oven to 350 degrees. Mix dry ingredients in a large bowl. In a medium-sized bowl, mix eggs, milk, oil, and vanilla. Mix well, then add pumpkin. Mix well and fold in dry ingredients. Add pine nuts. Pour batter into two greased 5-by-9-inch loaf pans and bake for 45 minutes.

Algonquin Wild Nut Soup

24 oz. hazelnuts, crushed
6 shallots with tops
3 tbsp. parsley, chopped
6 cups stock
1 tsp. salt
¼ tsp. black pepper

Place all ingredients in a large soup pot and simmer slowly over a medium heat for 1½ hours, stirring occasionally.

Preparation

In the weeks prior to the event, create and distribute fliers. Post fliers in the library and neighboring schools. Post program information on the library website.

Ask your Teen Advisory Board (if you have one) to create decorations, including a tepee that will be raffled off at the end of the day. During the day, it will be used to store various materials for the program. Decorations will also include cornhusks, raffia, tribal masks, beads, bow and arrows (up high, so they cannot be touched), rope, dried vegetables, etc.

Since the program is to be quite large in scale, the help of volunteers and members of the Friends organization is needed during the craft portions and food service. In order to keep the momentum of the program, cleanup in between events will be very quick and organized; trash cans and boxes will be readily available and accessible.

Cost and Materials

The costs for this program would be from $0 to $200 for up to thirty participants. However, if donations are made either in money or in-kind, the costs can be greatly reduced through the support of your Friends of the Library. Beads and string can be purchased in bulk from Oriental Trading Company (www.orientaltrading.com).

Craft Kits

- Dream catchers, $5.59 per dozen
- Pouch necklace, $5.99 per dozen
- Pony beads, $7.99 for 2,000
- Feathers, $4.99 for 800

Food

The budget for food will depend on support or donations from the Friends of the Library group and local restaurants. Approximate costs for sufficient quantities would be between $50 and $100; however, for libraries serving a larger community with an active Friends group, the budget could be expanded.

Bibliography

Alexie, Sherman. Illus. by Ellen Forney. *The Absolutely True Diary of a Part-Time Indian.* New York: Little, Brown, 2007.
> Junior, a budding cartoonist growing up on the Spokane Indian Reservation, is determined to take his future into his own hands. He leaves his troubled school on the rez to attend an all-white, farm-town high school where the only other Indian is the school mascot.

Alexie, Sherman. *Flight: A Novel.* New York: Grove/Atlantic, Black Cat, 2007.
> An orphaned and troubled teen learns the meaning of fear when he travels through time and in various bodies, and returns to himself forever changed. The story will make you laugh and cry.

Bruchac, Joseph. Illus. by Sally Wern Comport. *Bearwalker.* New York: Harper-Collins, 2007.

During a trip to the Adirondacks, Baron meets the bearlike creature in the Bearwalker legend, which he never thought to be real until now. The creature is more vicious than he ever imagined, and now he must help his classmates get free of the foreboding danger.

Bruchac, Joseph. *Geronimo.* New York: Scholastic Press, 2006.

Geronimo's life is nearing its end in a prison in Fort Sill, Oklahoma, in 1908. Geronimo lived through the horrors of many dangers and withstood bullet and knife wounds, demonstrating his stamina as one of the greatest of warriors and spiritual leaders of his time.

Bruchac, Joseph. *Skeleton Man.* New York: HarperCollins, 2001.

When Molly wakes up to find that her parents have vanished, she is turned over to the care of a mysterious great-uncle. She must rely on her dreams about the Skeleton Man from an old Mohawk story for her safety and a solution to the mystery.

Bruchac, James, and Joseph Bruchac. Illus. by Kayeri Akweks. *Native American Games and Stories.* Golden, CO: Fulcrum Kids, 2000.

Stories and games offered by acclaimed Native American authors.

Carlson, Lori M. *Moccasin Thunder: American Indian Stories for Today.* New York: HarperCollins, 2005.

Ten refreshing stories about Native American teens by authors such as Sherman Alexie, Cynthia Leitich Smith, and Joseph Bruchac.

Carson, Dale. *New Native American Cooking: More Than 125 Traditional Foods and Contemporary Dishes Made from America's Indigenous Ingredients.* New York: Random House, 1996.

Each recipe includes background information about how to prepare each dish. Includes menu-planning advice and ingredient substitutes. The author is a member of the Abenaki tribe.

Corwin, Judith Hoffman. *Native American Crafts of the Plains and Plateau.* New York: Franklin Watts, 2002.

Instructions are given for several enjoyable crafts of the Plains and Plateau Indian tribes, and they are described in terms of their historical significance.

Frank, Lois Ellen, and Cynthia J. Frank. *Native American Cooking: Foods of the Southwest Indian Nations.* New York: C. N. Potter, 1991.

More than eighty easy-to-prepare recipes rich in natural flavors and appropriate for today's healthy eating. The author, part Kiowa, collaborated with other tribesmen across the Southwest to provide the secrets to authentic Native American fare. Illustrated.

Juettner, Bonnie. *100 Native Americans Who Changed American History.* Milwaukee, WI: World Almanac Library, 2005.

Part of a series, this book features most famous Native Americans who have influenced American history. Each chapter presents a biography, important accomplishments, and historical contexts. Sherman Alexie, a Native American poet and novelist, is included.

Monaghan, Kathleen, and Hermon Joyner. *You Can Weave! Projects for Young Weavers.* Worcester, MA: Davis Publications, 2000.

A weaving book for kids with instructions for projects that actually work. Some of the projects are small pouches, mug rugs, rag placemats, two tapestry samplers, and a great ikat dyed belt. Illustrated.

Morris, Ting, Illus. by Emma Young. *Arts and Crafts of the Native Americans.* North Mankato, MN: Smart Apple Media, 2007.

A concise discussion of Native American handicrafts with simple instructions for completing a variety of projects.

Pollock, Penny. Illus. by Ed Young. *The Turkey Girl: A Zuni Cinderella Story.* Boston: Little, Brown, 1995.

Believing the Dance of the Sacred Bird to be a poor girl's event of a lifetime, a beautiful young turkey keeper fears that her tattered clothing and shabby appearance will keep her away, until her turkeys give her a beautiful feather gown.

Temko, Florence. Illus. by Randall Gooch. *Traditional Crafts from Native North America.* Culture Crafts series. Minneapolis, MN: Lerner, 1997.

This book gives straightforward instructions for creating simple North American Indian crafts.

The First Floridians: A Celebration of Florida's Native Americans

By Amanda Reid Peak

This program can be used as a prototype for librarians and media specialists in other states who could adapt it to their states.

Age Level

12–14 years

Duration of Library Program

One 50-minute period or more, or over a period of one week.

Overall Goal

The goal of this program is for sixth- through eighth-grade students who use the school media center to come to a better understanding of the rich history of the first Floridians, the Native American tribes who inhabited this area of the country.

The objective of this program is to present students with historical and cultural information about some of the most prevalent Native American tribes in Florida before the arrival of the Europeans, including the Tocobago tribe, which inhabited the Tampa Bay area. This program can last for up to five days, with an emphasis on a variety of adaptations of Native American culture, past and present, throughout the week.

This program is designed to be entertaining and fun, in order to capture the students' imaginations, but will be educational at the same time, so they learn about the people who lived in their state before them.

Relevance to the Community Served

This program is relevant to students who live in Florida, and it is important for them to know as much as possible about the vast history of their state. It is good for them to have an understanding that there was a large, vibrant culture in their state for thousands of years before the Spanish, French, and English arrived. There are still large Seminole populations in Florida, and it is important for people to learn about one another and respect the culture and history of the various ethnic groups who live in the state, including the Native Americans.

Activities

Some of the activities that will be included in this school library program on Florida Native Americans are samples of popular Native American foods (prepared by the media specialist and volunteers), a poster board with a map of Florida and the names of the most prevalent tribes placed in the areas they lived, a poster board of the great Seminole, Osceola, and his life and contribution to history, and copies of real photographs of Native Americans from the nineteenth century. The food will include corn on the cob, hominy—which was a favorite corn dish of the Seminole tribe (seasoned with butter and salt to appeal to modern tastes!)—traditional pumpkin bread cakes, oranges, and melon. This will be an attention-grabbing aspect of the program to give the participants a real "flavor" of life in Florida long ago.

The map of Florida poster board will include the names of Native American tribes, from each different area of Florida, including the Timucua tribe in the northeast, the Tequesta and Seminole tribes in the southeast, the Calusa tribe in the southwest, the Apalachee tribe in the northwest, and the Tocobago tribe in the Tampa Bay area. Other tribes included will be the Ais, Miccosukee, and Yemassee.

The famous Seminole Indian Osceola will be featured on a poster with information about his life and influence. This poster board will include pictures of Osceola and a chronology of his life, including the wars in which he was involved. (See "Additional Materials.") There will be many pictures of actual Native Americans from the nineteenth century displayed in order to garner interest in them as individual people, and for the students to see what they really looked like.

Preparation

Prepare the following materials to be included in this school library program:

- Handouts of annotated bibliographies including relevant websites for interested students' further education
- Handouts of a list of Native American words and place names that have been preserved by the common culture of Florida and the United States
- A fact sheet about some of the most famous Native Americans in the state
- A display of books containing information on Native Americans
- A promotional flier for the library program that will be hung throughout the school and in the library in the two weeks leading up to and during the Native American program
- Poster boards featuring a map of Florida tribes, Osceola, and photographs of nineteenth-century Florida Native Americans

The food items will be provided by the librarian and parent volunteers at their own expense.

- Corn dish of the Seminole tribe
- Traditional pumpkin bread cakes
- Oranges and melons

Cost and Materials

Approximate cost: $0–$160

The estimation of $160 is calculated based on the number of copies of the promotional fliers, photographs, poster boards, and handouts needed to reach a population of about four hundred students.

Bibliography

Andryszewski, Tricia. *The Seminoles: People of the Southeast.* Brookfield, CT: Millbrook Press, 1995.

> A book about the history of the Seminole tribe with much information about Seminoles of today, including many photographs.

Costabel, Eva Deutsch. *The Early People of Florida.* New York: Atheneum, 1993.

> A brief overview of the Native American tribes of Florida, as well as the first European explorers from Spain, France, and England.

Jumper, Betty Mae. Illus. by Guy LaBree. *Legends of the Seminoles*. Sarasota, FL: Pineapple Press, 1994.
> A collection of folktales and legends handed down orally from the Seminole tribe. Illustrated with original color paintings.

Koestler-Grack, Rachel A. *Osceola, 1804–1838*. Mankato, MN: Blue Earth Books, 2003.
> A brief life story of the life and times of Osceola the warrior, and the Seminole tribe.

Lawson, Edith Ridenour. Illus. by Mike Skeggs. *Florida Indians: Noble Redmen of the South*. St. Petersburg, FL: Valkyrie Press, 1977.
> An excellent overview of the history and culture of the various Native American tribes of Florida.

Webliography

Ancient Native. www.ancientnative.org.
> A site dedicated to preserving the history and heritage of the first people of Florida.

Exploring Florida; Social Studies Resources for Students and Teachers. "Native Americans in Florida gallery." http://fcit.usf.edu/florida/photos/native/native.htm.
> An interesting site with a large photo gallery of Florida Native Americans from the nineteenth century to today, archeological sites, and other items of interest.

Exploring Florida; Social Studies Resources for Students and Teachers. "Tocobaga Indians of Tampa Bay." http://fcit.usf.edu/florida/lessons/tocobag/tocobag1.htm.
> This site contains information on the Native Americans that lived in the Tampa Bay area.

Indigenous Peoples Literature. "Osceola, Seminole." www.indigenouspeople.net/osceola.htm.
> A good site about the life and times of the great Native American Seminole Osceola.

The Seminole Tribe of Florida. www.seminoletribe.com.
> A fact-filled and interesting site about the Seminole tribe of the past and today.

Additional Materials

Native American Vocabulary We Still Use Today!

Florida Place Names

Apalachicola—"Place of the ruling people"
Elfers—"Hunting grounds"

Kissimmee—"Winding water"
Miami—"Big water"
Ocala—"Spring"
Thonotosassa—"Flint place"
Weeki Wachee—"Small spring"

American Indian Words in Use Today
moccasin

tobacco

succotash

tomato

chocolate

hammock

hurricane

Osceola and the Seminole Tribe

The Seminoles are actually Creek Native Americans who broke away from their own tribes in order to avoid conflict with Europeans. They left Alabama and Georgia in order to find freedom in Florida.

These Native Americans did find freedom for a short while in Florida, but the new U.S. government, with General Andrew Jackson in control, was determined to stop them. He marched across Florida, burning Native American towns along the way, to settle what he called the "Indian problem." This is known as the First Seminole War.

Osceola, the great Seminole leader, was born in Alabama in 1804. His name means "black drink," which was a popular drink that was supposed to cleanse the body and spirit.

In 1835 he stabbed his knife into the treaty he was asked to sign that would move his people from their swamplands in southeast Florida to territories west of the Mississippi. This led to the Second Seminole War.

Osceola was tricked into discussing peace and was captured in 1837 while carrying a white flag of truce. He was imprisoned in Fort Moultrie, South Carolina, where he soon died of fever.

Today, more than two thousand Seminoles live on six Florida reservations, which are located in Hollywood, Big Cypress, Brighton, Immokalee, Ft. Pierce, and Tampa. They never signed a peace treaty, and the Seminole have always been an independent nation.

The Native Americans of Tampa Bay

The Tocobago lived in the northern part of the Tampa Bay area from 900 to 1500 AD. They lived in small villages surrounding a public area that was used as a meeting place. The houses were round huts made with wooden poles and palm thatches.

The Tocobago built burial mounds in which they buried their dead. They also placed their tribal chief's house and temples on top of mounds. The women of the tribes made their own mounds of discarded shells and other garbage, called *middens.*

The Tocobago ate fish, shellfish and the then-abundant manatee. They also ate deer, rabbits, squirrels, and armadillos, as well as berries, nuts, and fruit. They even traded with northern tribes for corn.

Around 1528, the Spanish explorer Panfilo de Narvaez arrived in Tampa Bay and brought disease and violence to the Tocobago Native Americans. Within one hundred years, they were extinct.

Mesoamerican Culture: The Mayan Civilization

By Sarah Jünke

Age Level

12–14 years

Duration of Library Program

Approximately 90 minutes

Introduction and Background

The peoples who would later become known as American Indians are thought to have crossed into North America from Asia between eleven thousand and thirty thousand years ago, eventually spreading across North, Central, and South America. Many prominent civilizations developed in Central and South America, including the Aztec, Olmec, Toltec, Inca, and Maya. Archaeologists have found remnants of early Mayan villages dating back to 2000 BC. The Mayan culture grew from these villages to become a vast Mesoamerican civilization, with many city-states stretching from southern Mexico to the modern Central American countries of Guatemala, Honduras,

El Salvador, and Belize. Mayan culture gave the Western hemisphere its first fully developed system of writing, and also contributed greatly in astronomy, art, mathematics, and architecture. The Mayan civilization saw a decline in 1450 and eventually was conquered by the Spanish in 1697, after 170 years of attempts at subjugation. The Mayan people and culture did not disappear, though, and over six million Maya still live in the countries of Guatemala, Mexico, and Belize.

Overall Goal

The objective is to learn about the ancient Native American civilization known as the Maya and to appreciate the heritage of modern-day Maya.

This program will enrich the understanding and appreciation of Native American cultures that students learn about in history classes. This program is targeted at middle school students and can be offered in a school media center or public library.

Relevance to the Community Served

This program is relevant to middle school students because it will help them to learn about the history of the great civilization established by the native people who once lived on this American continent where the students now live. This theme is also relevant to middle school history and social science curricula.

Overview

This program will include four activities covering Mayan history and culture, food, folktales, and the modern Maya. As a tie-in for the program, the library should set up a display featuring images of Mayan art, culture, and books about ancient and modern Mayan civilization.

Activities

Activity 1: Mayan History and Culture (15–20 minutes)

Using the background information provided, and resources in the "Bibliography" and "Webliography" sections, compose a presentation about the history and culture of the Maya. Include information about their origin, geographic area covered, time line, urbanism, agriculture, writing, artwork, architecture, religion, astronomy, mathematics, trade, and decline. This website offers vast amounts of information: www.jaguar-sun.com.

Activity 2: Mayan Food (10–20 minutes)

Choose one or two different kinds of food listed below. You may have food prepared ahead of time if it needs to be cooked, or if using uncooked dishes, you can have the participants assemble. Consult resources listed under the "Bibliography" or "Webliography" sections, or use the ideas below. Tell the participants about the food and its relevance to the Maya, and then serve the food or let the participants assemble it. The food can be eaten during the next activity to save time.

Popcorn

Corn was a vital staple of the Mayan diet and was highly valued and considered sacred. Corn is still important to the modern Maya and comprises the majority of caloric intake for some communities. Popcorn was eaten by the Maya and would be a fun and easy food to prepare. (Use microwave popcorn or a popcorn machine.)

Hot Chocolate

The Maya also prepared and ate chocolate. Hot chocolate was popular and sometimes included chili pepper to add spice. (Use microwave hot chocolate or boil water in an electric kettle or coffee machine, then add to chocolate in cups.)

Vanilla

Vanilla was another common crop in Mayan agriculture. The recipe for vanilla-fruit compote found at http://car.utsa.edu/Legacy/mayarecipes.htm uses vanilla and fruits that would have been eaten by the ancient Maya. (This should be made ahead of time, as it requires a stove.)

Other Mayan Foodstuffs

Squash, beans, chili pepper, yucca, tomato, avocado, guava, papaya, pineapple, pumpkin, sweet potato, allspice.

Activity 3: Mayan folktales (20–30 minutes)

Select some folktales from the resources provided in the "Bibliography" and "Webliography" sections and copy them onto handouts to distribute to the participants. Let them take turns reading the folktales to the group. With each folktale, include some information that puts it into context and explains its relevance to Mayan culture.

Activity 4: Modern Maya (10–20 minutes)

Many of the pre-Columbian civilizations in the Americas were decimated by Spanish conquest, and their ways of life were lost or subsumed by Spanish culture. The Mayan culture did not disappear though, and over six million Maya still live in Central America. Spanish culture influenced the Maya, and today they follow a religion of Catholicism mixed with ancient beliefs and traditions. The modern Maya have been frequently caught in the middle of warfare and suppression and have been attacked in Guatemala and Chiapas, Mexico. This website provides a good introduction to the modern Maya with accompanying resources: www.jaguar-sun.com/mayanow.html. Further resources can be found in the "Bibliography" and "Webliography" sections.

For this activity, provide the participants with some information about the culture and plight of the modern Maya, either through handouts or a brief discussion. Offer a list of resources and books about the modern Maya.

Preparation

- Handouts/discussion points for the activities need to be prepared, particularly for activities 1, 3, and 4.
- Food ingredients need to be procured and the food needs to be prepared ahead of time or set up for preparation during the program.
- The program should be advertised through various outlets, including the library's bulletin board, newsletter, website, Facebook and MySpace, and other communication vehicles. For public libraries, include fliers at local venues including coffee shops and bookstores.
- Procurement of Mayan civilization books and images for display
- Setup of Mayan culture display in library

Cost and Materials

Approximate cost: $0–$50

- Ingredients for food (acquire through donations or purchase)
- Cookware for food
- Plates, cups, napkins, etc.
- Paper, printing for handouts
- Mayan culture books

Bibliography

Crosher, Judith. *Technology in the Time of the Maya.* Austin, TX: Raintree Steck-Vaughn, 1998.
> Book about ancient Mayan material culture and technology. Projects are included.

Day, Nancy. *Your Travel Guide to Ancient Mayan Civilization.* Minneapolis, MN: Runestone Press, 2001.
> Introduction to Mayan culture from 600 to 800 AD. Includes information about geography and economy as well as games, trivia, and recipes. Black-and-white and color photos.

Galvin, Irene Flum. *The Ancient Maya.* New York: Benchmark Books, 1997.
> Descriptions of Mayan art, poetry, religion, language, astronomy, and daily life.

Mikaelsen, Ben. *Tree Girl.* New York: HarperCollins/HarperTempest, 2004.
> The story of a modern Maya girl, Gabriela, is based on a true story. Gabriela is witness to a terrible massacre in her village.

Sexton, James D. *Mayan Folktales: Folklore from Lake Atitlán, Guatemala.* New York: Anchor Books, 1992.
> Thirty-five folktales representative of Mayan mythic heritage.

Talbert, Marc. *Heart of a Jaguar.* New York: Simon and Schuster Books for Young Readers, 1995.
> The story of a teenage boy in the ancient Mayan city of Chichen Itza who is dealing with becoming an adult during a time of drought and despair.

Webliography

Arte Maya Tz'utuhi. "Paintings of Corn—Maize." www.artemaya.com/contmaiz.html.
> Images depicting the importance of corn in Mayan life.

Giese, Paula. "Maya Culture." www.kstrom.net/isk/maya/mayastor.html.
> Stories from Mayan heritage as told by modern Maya.

Jaguar-Sun. "Archaeology of the Ancient Mayan Civilization of Mesoamerica." www.jaguar-sun.com.
> Extensive resource on ancient Mayan culture and modern Maya. Contains links to other resources.

Maya World Studies Center. "Maya Calendar." http://mayacalendar.com/mayacalendar.html.
> Information about the Mayan calendar as well as other topics such as mathematics.

Mayaweb. "Culture and History of the Ancient and Modern Maya." http://home.kpn.nl/roeli049/enghome1.htm.
> Information about ancient and modern Maya. Includes a tool to write your name in hieroglyphics.

National Gallery of Art. "Courtly Art of the Ancient Maya." www.nga.gov/exhibitions/2004/maya/lifeatcourt.shtm.

Images and description of ancient Mayan artwork.

ThinkQuest. "The Maya Explorer." http://library.thinkquest.org/C004577/home.php3.

Information about ancient Mayan civilization, including society, mathematics, calendar, language, astronomy, religion, and cities. Includes an interactive quiz.

TravelYucatan.com. "Meet the Modern Maya." www.travelyucatan.com/maya/meet_the_modern_maya.php.

Provides information about the modern Maya, as well as profiles of Mayan people.

University of Austin. "Maya Recipes." http://car.utsa.edu/Legacy/mayarecipes.htm.

Mayan recipes including hot chocolate, honey-vanilla fruit compote, new corn–stuffed tamales, pumpkin soup, *keh chuuc,* and more.

CHAPTER 5

Cross-Cultural Programming

The Wonderful World of Cinderella

By Stephanie G. Stover

Age Level

10–14 years

Duration of Library Program

2½ hours

Introduction and Background

Almost everyone is aware of the traditional Cinderella tale. The library wants to promote cultural awareness in the community by featuring a few of the more than three hundred Cinderella stories known throughout the world.

Overall Goal

The goal is to provide awareness of other cultures by using a familiar, almost universal story. The objective is to have an audience of teens and tweens become interested and aware that there are other cultures in the world that have their own versions.

Relevance to the Community Served

Teens and tweens will be introduced to other cultures through the telling of these multicultural Cinderella stories. This program is relevant to younger teens who are beginning to open their eyes to multiple cultures around them. They should develop sensitivity toward cultural diversity through understanding the similarities and differences across different cultures, which can be effectively presented by reading the familiar Cinderella story delivered in culturally different versions.

Activities

At the start of the program, welcome the audience to the library, and introduce them to the Cinderella story. Read the five featured Cinderella stories aloud:

> *Cendrillon: A Cajun Cinderella* by Sheila Herbert Collins
> *Yeh-Shen: A Cinderella Story from China* by Ai-Ling Louie
> *The Persian Cinderella* by Shirley Climo
> *The Irish Cinderlad* by Shirley Climo
> *Adelita: A Mexican Cinderella Story* by Tomie dePaola

After finishing the readings and discussion, use a wall map of the world to identify where each of the featured Cinderella tales originated. Ask students to tack a glass slipper cut-out onto the world map to locate where each story originated:

> *The Irish Cinderlad*
> *The Korean Cinderella*
> *The Persian Cinderella*
> *Cendrillon: A Cajun Cinderella*
> *Yeh-Shen: A Cinderella Story from China*
> *Adelita: A Mexican Cinderella Story*
> *The Egyptian Cinderella*
> *Abadeha: The Philippine Cinderella*
> *The Gift of the Crocodile: A Cinderella Story* (Indonesian)
> *The Way Meat Loves Salt: A Cinderella Tale from Jewish Tradition*
> *Smoky Mountain Rose: An Appalachian Cinderella*
> *The Golden Sandal: A Middle Eastern Cinderella Story*
> *Little Gold Star: A Spanish American Cinderella Tale*
> *Fair, Brown, and Trembling: An Irish Cinderella Story*

Sootface: An Ojibwa Cinderella Story

The Rough-Face Girl (Algonquin Tribe)

Introduce a brief language lesson featuring French, Chinese, Persian, Spanish, and Gaelic. (Only French, Spanish, and Gaelic will be practiced.) Start with *Cendrillon: A Cajun Cinderella,* which has many French words in the text. Then introduce other words from other languages. Volunteers who are able to speak these languages will be present to teach the participants a few of the words that are used in these cultures. Take-home flash cards will be passed out to the audience after the words are introduced.

Follow with a discussion of the Cinderella most familiar to Americans as compared to the Chinese and Persian versions, also a discussion of the Irish Cinderella and its differences and similarities.

And finally, for the Mexican Cinderella story, there will be a cookbook created with recipes, and a piñata filled with toys and candy. Have participants create a recipe booklet, and break open the piñata.

Preparation

- Locate multilingual volunteers to assist with the language lesson.
- Find all of the library's Cinderella titles and purchase any additional ones that are needed.
- Get donations for the piñata, or make one, along with all of the prizes and candy that would be placed inside.
- Locate recipes; photocopy them, landscape orientation, two per page; and fold and staple pages to form a book. Recipes included will be featured in a table of contents on the first page, and covers can be participants' drawings from the Mexican Cinderella story. Foods in the recipe book will include easy-to-make recipes such as sapodillas, tacos, salsa, beans, quesadillas, and plantains.
- The piñata will be hung in a tree outside the library, or the location can be adapted depending on space. For safety reasons, no one can begin until the whistle is blown and the leader hollers, *"Arriba,"* meaning it is safe to start. Err on the side of caution to prevent stampeding. Inform participants of the rules and have prizes available for less aggressive players.
- Prepare an area for a wall map of the world. Use a world map free of copyright found at CIA.gov and donated by Friends of the Library.

- Draw and cut out multiple images of a glass slipper for the wall map activity.
- Create a flier with an RSVP, so that enough supplies will be on hand.
- Have all art supplies donated and flash cards donated.

Cost and Materials

Approximate cost: $0–$50

Many supplies can be donated for this program.

- Handouts
- Fliers
- Wall map
- Recipes and other booklets
- Piñata and candy

Bibliography

Climo, Shirley. Illus. by Ruth Heller. *The Egyptian Cinderella*. New York: Crowell, 1989.

In the Egyptian version of Cinderella set in the sixth century BC, a slave girl is chosen by the pharaoh to be the next queen.

Climo, Shirley. Illus. by Loretta Krupinski. *The Irish Cinderlad*. New York: HarperCollins, 1996.

Set in Ireland, a boy mistreated by his stepmother leaves home, fends off a sea serpent, and rescues a princess.

Climo, Shirley. Illus. by Ruth Heller. *The Korean Cinderella*. New York: HarperCollins, 1993.

Cinderella set in ancient Korea. Pear Blossom, suffering mistreatment by her stepmother, eventually is chosen to be the queen by the king.

Climo, Shirley. Illus. by Robert Florczak. *The Persian Cinderella*. New York: HarperCollins, 1999.

Set in Persia, Settareh is mistreated by her stepfamily, and finds magic in a blue jug.

Collins, Sheila Herbert. Illus. by Patrick Soper. *Cendrillon: A Cajun Cinderella*. New York: Pelican, 1998.

A Cajun variant of the Cinderella tale set in New Orleans, in which the ball is held during Mardi Gras.

Daly, Jude. *Fair, Brown and Trembling: An Irish Cinderella Story*. New York: Farrar, Straus, and Giroux, 2000.

An Irish folktale about Cinderella overcoming her stepmother and stepsisters' wickedness.

De La Paz, Myrna J. Illus. by You-shan Tang. *Abadeha: The Philippine Cinderella.* Auburn, CA: Shen's Books, 2001.

> Set in the Philippines, this Cinderella is helped by the Spirit of the Forest to marry the chieftain's son.

dePaola, Tomie. *Adelita: A Mexican Cinderella Story.* New York: G. P. Putnam's Sons, 2002.

> Set in Mexico, Adelita is an orphan being raised by her cruel stepmother. She meets her prince at a grand fiesta.

Hickox, Rebecca. Illus. by Will Hillenbrand. *The Golden Sandal: A Middle Eastern Cinderella.* New York: Holiday House, 1998.

> This is an Iraqi story of Cinderella, where she is helped by a magical red fish. She gets golden sandals for the ball.

Jaffe, Nina. Illus. by Louise August. *The Way Meat Loves Salt: A Cinderella Tale from the Jewish Tradition.* New York: Henry Holt and Company, 1998.

> After being sent away from her home, this Cinderella is aided by the prophet Elijah, who helps her to marry a scholar's son. Includes translations and a Yiddish wedding song.

Louie, Ai-Ling. Illus. by Ed Young. *Yeh-Shen: A Cinderella Story from China.* New York: Philomel Books, 1982.

> Yeh-Shen is mistreated by her stepmother. Her stepmother kills her only friend, a fish, whose bones Yeh-Shen uses for magic. She has golden slippers to wear to the ball.

Martin, Rafe. Illus. by David Shannon. *The Rough-Face Girl.* New York: G. P. Putnam's Sons, 1992.

> An Algonquin Cinderella story where Cinderella and her sisters have to be able to see the Invisible Man and his bow and string if they want to marry him.

San Souci, Robert D. Illus. by Brian Pinkney. *Cendrillon: A Caribbean Cinderella.* New York: Simon and Schuster Books for Young Readers, 1998.

> A Creole variance of the Cinderella story, set in New Orleans. Has French in the text with translations.

San Souci, Robert D. Illus. by David Catrow. *Cinderella Skeleton.* San Diego: Harcourt/Silver Whistle, 2000.

> A unique Cinderella story where the main characters are skeletons. The story is set to a rhymed retelling of the story of a young woman who finds her prince at a Halloween ball.

San Souci, Robert D. Illus. by Sergio Martinez. *Little Gold Star: A Spanish American Cinderella Tale.* New York: HarperCollins, 2000.

> A Spanish American version of Cinderella story featuring the Virgin Mary as the fairy godmother.

San Souci, Robert D. Illus. by Daniel San Souci. *Sootface: An Ojibwa Cinderella Story.* New York: Delacorte, 1994.

> An American Indian version of Cinderella story. An Ojibwa girl is mistreated

by her two older sisters. All of the village girls want to marry a mighty invisible hunter across the river, but an Indian girl wins him for her husband with her kind and honest heart.

Schroeder, Alan. Illus. by Brad Sneed. *Smoky Mountain Rose: An Appalachian Cinderella.* New York: Dial Books for Young Readers, 1997.

Set in the Appalachian Mountains, this Cinderella is aided by a magical pig to get to the ball. This book features wonderful illustrations by Brad Sneed.

Sierra, Judy. Illus. by Reynold Ruffins. *The Gift of the Crocodile: A Cinderella Story.* New York: Simon and Schuster Books for Young Readers, 2000.

Set in Indonesia, a girl named Damura escapes her cruel stepmother and stepsister and is aided by Grandmother Crocodile, who helps her marry the prince.

Additional Materials

Language Learning from Multicultural Cinderella Stories

French

hello	bonjour
goodbye	au revior
please	s'il vous plait
no	non
yes	oui
prince	prince

Korean

hello	안녕하세요 (an-nyŏng-ha-se-yo)
goodbye	안녕히 가세요 (an-nyŏng-hi-ga-se-yo)
please	제발 (chebal);
	해 주시겠어요 (hae-ju-si-ge-ssŭ-yo)
no	아니요 (a-ni-yo)
yes	예 (ye)
prince	왕자 (wang-ja)

Persian

hello	سلام (salām)
goodbye	خدا حافظ (khodā hāfez)
please	لطفآ (lotfan)
no	نه (na)
yes	بله (bale)
prince	شاهز اده (shahzadeh)

Spanish

hello	hola
goodbye	adiós
please	por favor
no	no
yes	sí
prince	príncipe

Gaelic

hello	hoigh
goodbye	slan
please	le do thoil
no	anon; ar bith
yes	is es anois
prince	prionsa
princess	banphrionsa

Discussion of Cinderella Stories

Discussion of the differences between the traditional Cinderella story and the Cinderella stories *Yeh-Shen* and *The Persian Cinderella*.

1. Who are the main characters?
2. Where does each Cinderella live?
3. Who helps Cinderella?
4. How does Cinderella get to the ball?
5. How does the prince find her?
6. How are these Cinderella stories different from the Cinderella story that you know?
7. What type of shoe does each Cinderella wear?

Multicultural Readers Program
By Eleonora Fieitas

Age Level
12–13 years

Duration of Library Program
3 months

Introduction and Background
The goal of the program is to promote reading as well as awareness of other cultures in students ages 12 through 13.

Chosen cultures: The program will contain books on African American, Japanese, Native American, Dominican Republican, Hispanic, Jewish, Muslim, Chinese, and Korean cultures. Since the goal of the program is to increase multicultural appreciation, a variety of cultures are included. The program will incorporate literature, traditional costumes, and traditional food from these cultures.

Overall Goal

The Multicultural Readers program will foster an appreciation of different cultures.

The program will promote students' reading of multicultural literature. Circulation of multicultural materials will increase as a result. Students will also become more familiar with the various cultures presented in the program.

Relevance to the Community Served

This reading program is relevant for students in the sixth through seventh grades who should broaden their scope and understanding of different cultures in their comprehension of the world in which they live. Through the exposure to a variety of multicultural readings, the participants will gain a better understanding of the world and people around them.

Activities

Students and teachers will check out books from the list of titles included in the program. Teachers will fill out Certificate of Reading forms for their students or class to indicate which books each student has read. Students will bring these forms to the media center, where the titles read will be checked off on a bulletin board displaying classes and/or students. Each time a student or class reads three books, a small treat such as a pencil, eraser, bookmark, no-homework coupon, or pizza coupon will be given.

Once a student has read all nine books, he will be invited to attend the Voting Party. At the Voting Party, students will be able to vote on their favorite book of the program. Students will also taste foods and dress in costumes from the different cultures portrayed in the program. The winning title will be showcased in the media center and awarded the school Multicultural Book of the Year Award.

Preparation

Prior to starting the program, there are several tasks that must be completed. First, the media specialist must secure approval to conduct the program from the administration. Next, copies of the titles introduced in the program will be ordered. (Refer to the bibliography for the list of titles.)

Create photocopies of the informational fliers. The media specialist may also request to speak at a faculty meeting to pass out the fliers to teachers and discuss the program with them.

Student informational fliers must be photocopied and distributed. Student treats should be prepared or purchased.

Make copies of the Certificate of Reading forms to distribute to teachers.

Once these steps have been completed, display the titles on a bookshelf by the entrance of the media center to encourage participation. Set up a bulletin board with student treats and Classroom Reading Logs that will showcase students who are participating in the program.

Make arrangements for the multicultural food for the Voting Party with the Parent Teacher Association.

Make copies of the reminder flier, the invitations, and the ballots at the beginning of February.

Fliers will be sent out two weeks prior to the completion of the program to encourage students to finish reading all nine books. Invitations will be sent out to those students who read all nine titles.

Cost and Materials

Approximate cost: $0–$300

- Books (at least thirty copies of each) if library does not already own them. If more copies are needed, these can be purchased with library budget monies or via a small grant (such as Tolerance.org via Southern Poverty Law Center), or from Friends of the Library donations. Costs for the purchase of all books would be estimated at approximately $2,700. Later, these books can be developed into kits that can be circulated among teachers for their classes.
- Pencils, erasers, bookmarks, and other treats. Also, creation or purchase of no-homework coupons, pizza coupons, etc.

Local restaurants, office supply stores, and the Parent Teacher Association may make donations to assist with funding. Also, school book fair profits may also be used as a source of funding. In addition, on the informational flier sent home with students, there may be a request for parents to make donations of books for the program.

Bibliography

Alvarez, Julia. *Before We Were Free.* New York: Knopf, 2002.

Author Julia Alvarez tells a story about the adolescence, perseverance, and struggle of Anita de la Torre, a twelve-year-old girl who fled the Dominican Republic with her family for freedom.

Anaya, Rudolfo A. *Bless Me, Ultima.* **New York: Warner Books, 1994.**

This story of a young boy is set in New Mexico in the 1940s. When the visitor Ultima, a *curandera* (a traditional folk healer who cures people with herbs and magic) comes into his life, Antonio's eyes are gradually opened to his bonds with his culture and stories of the past.

Curtis, Christopher Paul. *Elijah of Buxton.* **New York: Scholastic Press, 2007.**

The story of a boy who happened to be the first child born free in a town called Buxton, Canada, a settlement of runaway slaves near the American border, in 1859. Despite his symbolic image, he is a fragile and talkative young boy. Everything changes when a former slave steals money from Elijah's friend and Elijah's dangerous journey begins. He becomes a hero by using his wits and skills and brings justice back to the town.

Hudson, Jan. *Sweetgrass.* **New York: Philomel Books, 1989.**

This historical novel vividly illustrates the culture of the Dakota Indians in the 1830s. Living on the western Canadian prairie, Sweetgrass, a fifteen-year-old Blackfoot Indian girl, wants to marry a young warrior, Eagle-Sun, but her father thinks she is too young. Then, after she saves her family from many difficulties, including natural disasters, a smallpox epidemic, and conflicts with white settlers, Sweetgrass convinces her father of her maturity.

Kadohata, Cynthia. *Kira-kira.* **New York: Atheneum Books for Young Readers, 2004.**

Chronicles a friendship between Katie and Lynn, two Japanese American sisters growing up in rural Georgia during the late 1950s and early 1960s. Lynn teaches her younger sister a special way of seeing the world and the hope for the brighter future. As despair falls upon the family when Lynn becomes fatally ill, Katie reminds them all that there is always something glittering in the future.

Kent, Rose. *Kimchi and Calamari.* **New York: HarperCollins, 2007.**

This story tells eighth-grader Joseph's self-discoveries about race and family after his social studies teacher assigns an essay on cultural heritage and tracing the past. Joseph was born in Korea, but was adopted by an Italian American family when he was a baby. When Joseph must write an essay on his heritage, he struggles with his desire to locate his birth mother, his concern for his hard-working adoptive parents, and his own need to find himself and his identity.

Laird, Elizabeth. *Kiss the Dust.* **New York: Dutton Children's Books, 1992.**

A refugee story told through the eyes of a thirteen-year-old Iraqi girl. As the Iraqi secret police look for her father for his involvement with the Kurdish resistance movement, Tara Hawrami and her family leave their home to live in a brutal refugee camp.

Lowry, Lois. *Number the Stars*. Boston: Houghton Mifflin. 1989.

This Newbery Medal Book tells a story of a ten-year-old Danish girl and how her bravery and courage are tested when she helps her Jewish best friend, who is threatened by Nazis in Copenhagen in 1943.

Yep, Laurence. *Dragonwings*. New York: Harper and Row, 1975.

In the early twentieth century, Moon Shadow, an eight-year-old Chinese boy, sails to San Francisco from China to join his father, Windrider, who makes his living doing laundry. Father, with the help of his son, is willing to endure the mockery of the other Chinese and makes his dream come true. Moon Shadow's love and respect for his father grow, and finally he helps his father realize his dream of making a flying machine.

Multicultural Research and Creative Writing

By Melanie McCartney

Age Level
12–14 years

Duration of Library Program
4 to 8 weeks; 60-minute weekly sessions

Introduction and Background
Through this research-based creative writing program, students will acquire needed research and documentation skills, learn about cultures around the world, and articulate their thoughts and ideas in written form. Students are given the freedom to choose what culture they would like to research.

Overall Goal
The goal is to increase knowledge and awareness of different cultures; develop research skills and correctly cite sources; and analyze, evaluate, and synthesize cultural facts from research to write a creative fictional story.

Relevance to the Community Served

It is important for students in the sixth through eighth grades to develop a sound understanding of a variety of research methods, along with appropriate documentation skills. The ability to broaden their scope and understanding of different cultures is paramount in their comprehension of the world in which they live. Through analyzing, evaluating, and synthesizing information, students actively participate in the learning process. Students will share their written stories, which include cultural traditions, family values, religious values, history, and geography. Each will gain a better understanding of the world and people around them.

Activities

The librarian initiates the program by reading selections from *Nightjohn* and *Sing to the Sun*. Students will then choose cultures to research. After making their selections, they will be given a worksheet to write down research questions, which will help them explore their culture of interest. Questions they ask will direct their research process. Each student will be required to use the following resources: books, magazines or journals, and Internet resources. A cultural research form (see "Additional Materials") will be handed out to direct the process of research and documentation. After filling out the form, the students will be able to complete their assignments by writing a creative short story as their final product. The librarian is encouraged to solicit input from a creative writing teacher to develop detailed directions for the students.

Preparation

The school media specialist will need an adequate collection of multicultural literature and research sources. *National Geographic* will be one magazine source available. Students will be able to research through electronic databases such as ProQuest. Cultural research form will direct student progress and documentation skills. The media specialist will acquire an example of a mind map to give students a way to organize their thoughts. Students will write stories and share with classmates.

Cost and Materials

Approximate cost: $0–$30 for printed handouts and worksheets (more if books need to be ordered)

Bibliography

Bryan, Ashley. *Sing to the Sun: Poems and Pictures.* New York: HarperCollins, 1992.
    Ashley Bryan's collection of poems and paintings celebrates all aspects of
    life and the unique African American culture. Beautifully illustrated.
Paulsen, Gary. *Nightjohn.* New York: Delacorte, 1993.
    The brutal life of Sarny, a twelve-year-old slave girl, becomes more danger-
    ous when Nightjohn, who entered into the Waller plantation as a new slave,
    teaches her how to read and Sarny takes the risk to learn.

Webliography

CIA World Factbook. https://www.cia.gov/library/publications/the-world
    -factbook/index.html.
Library of Congress. "Portals to the World." www.loc.gov/rr/international/
    portals.html.
New York Times. "World Online." www.nytimes.com/pages/world/index
    .html.
Pearl K Wise Library. www.cpsd.us/crls/library/.

Additional Materials

CULTURAL RESEARCH FORM

1. What country and culture are you going to do your research on?

2. What specific information are you going to search for? List some keywords that may be helpful when beginning your research.
   a.
   b.
   c.
   d.
   e.

3. What are three different possible resources to find your information?
   a.
   b.
   c.

4. Where will you find these resources?

5. Create note cards to document sources and specific facts during your research process. Organize note cards into subjects listed below:
   cultural traditions
   family values
   religious traditions
   history
   geography

6. Organize your information into a logical format.

7. Using the facts obtained, create a fictional story.

8. Read your story and state your feelings about the writing you produced.

9. Describe how you feel about the information seeking and documentation process you went through to create your product. What would you change or do differently? What worked well for you?

Quilt Recollections

By Tamara Sines

Age Level
12–17 years

Duration of Library Program
The storyteller presentation will last approximately one and a half hours. There will be follow-up meetings targeting two different age groups. The two follow-up meetings for ages 12 and 13 will take about an hour and a half long each, totaling three hours.

The three follow-up meetings for ages 14 through 17 will vary in length. The first meeting will last around an hour. The last two meetings will be one to two hours long, depending on the number of teens and the amount of effort they want to put into their quilt. The optional meeting will be similar to a reception and only last thirty to forty-five minutes.

Introduction and Background

The program's focus is on quilts. Quilts are functional crafts made out of scraps, old clothes, and even burlap, and are used throughout different cultures for bedding. Many cultures have used quilts not only for bedding, but also for expressing family history, memories, stories, and even maps.

The program will not focus on any particular society; it will be inclusive of many cultures.

It is believed that African Americans used quilts as maps during the days of the Underground Railroad. Each symbol instructed, warned, or notified traveling slaves on where to go and how to proceed along their turbulent journey to freedom. Other cultures, including the Native Americans and the Hmong people, have used quilts to tell their society's struggles and triumphs. People from many backgrounds use quilts to remember. The memory may be that of a family tradition, a belief, or a simple memory of one's favorite shirt.

Overall Goal

This program will provide an outlet for tweens and teens to learn more about other cultures through functional crafts.

Relevance to the Community Served

The program is relevant to tweens and teens as it weaves various subjects, such as history, art, literature, and math, into the workmanship of quilting. Learning about quilts and working together with adults on making quilts will offer them a valuable hands-on experience to cultivate deeper appreciation, tolerance, and understanding toward other cultures and older generations.

Overview

The program will include a presentation and actual quilting. The series provides tweens and teens an opportunity to work with elders from their community. The program will incorporate math, art, literature and history. All of this offers the young patron the opportunity to cultivate appreciation and tolerance toward other cultures and the art of quilting.

Types of activities include

1. Storyteller presentation
2. Two follow-up activities for ages 12 and 13
3. Three follow-up activities for ages 14 through 17

Activities

The Storyteller Presentation

The Quilt Recollections program will begin with all ages being invited for a presentation. The storyteller will give a performance on the Underground Railroad, including a discussion of the use and the controversy surrounding quilts during this time period.

Other options for this program:

- Library staff performs and discusses quilting through the ages
- Invite a local professor to discuss cultural uses of quilting
- Invite a quilter to discuss the history of quilting or her own personal quilting story

Follow-up Meetings for Ages 12–13

Participants in the younger age group will meet one week after the presentation for their first follow-up meeting. Participants will have already read *The Keeping Quilt* by Patricia Polacco and *The Quilt* by Ann Jonas. There will be a discussion that will stress important memories, family traditions, and new experiences. Each participant will make two 9-by-9-inch paper squares that will be assembled into a wall quilt. Each tween/teen can personalize her squares by writing a memory, a new experience, or a family tradition within the squares. When all are finished, the young patrons will create a nine quilt block pattern and a flower pattern.

This group will meet one more time to read *Dia's Story Cloth: The Hmong People's Journey of Freedom* by Dia Cha. (This may need to be shortened depending on the age and attention span of the group being serviced.) They will then complete any unfinished squares. This will also be when the final step will occur, which will be to assemble the quilt onto a bulletin board for public viewing. Students will be invited to bring their family members in for a small reception, giving them an opportunity to share their blocks with family.

Follow-up Meetings for Ages 14–17

At their first meeting, this group will also discuss *The Keeping Quilt* by Patricia Polacco. Even though this is a picture book, it is a good way to illustrate what a quilt is and its many uses. They will have the opportunity to discuss any books on quilting they may have read as well as view websites about quilting. During this first meeting, the teens will be introduced to the members of the quilting guild that has volunteered its services for this project. Different methods of quilting will be discussed. The teens will be given a "homework assignment": they are to decide if they plan on drawing their chosen memory using fabric crayons or transfer a photograph onto cloth which could be further embellished.

In the next meeting, teens will transfer of their memories onto cloth. The teens will either draw their own memory or transfer their pictures with the use of the computer and the transfer sheets. For those who finish early, the guild members will begin to show them the quick tying method.

At the third meeting, teens will finish putting the pieces together into a quilt, followed by a discussion of the whole project. The teens may opt to have a final meeting to celebrate with friends and family the completion and displaying of their quilt. The guild members will sew the batting and the backing on the quilt.

Preparation

The library staff will assist as needed. The quilting guild will volunteer to cut the required fabric squares and fabric for the teen quilt. The library staff will preview appropriate websites and place on hold any other information required for the program.

The library staff will create fliers informing teens about the event. Fliers will be displayed within the library as well as around the community. They will also be given to all local schools to be displayed and handed out to students. The library will run an ad with the event information in numerous community papers. The annotated bibliography below will be given to the participants.

Cost and Materials

Approximate cost: $0–$100 (may be exceeded if there are more than thirty participants)

Supplies: *The Keeping Quilt* by Patricia Polacco, *The Quilt* by Ann Jonas, *Dia's Story Cloth: The Hmong People's Journey of Freedom* by Dia Cha, computer, construction paper, scissors, glue, fabric, fabric scissors, needles, thread, batting, fabric crayons, iron transfers, food for the receptions, advertisement.

Potential ways to save money:

- Ask the storyteller to provide a free program.
- Use picture books that are part of the library collection.
- Construction paper, scissors, and glue are normal stock items.

- Ask patrons and your local quilting guild to donate food, fabric, needles, thread, and fabric scissors.
- The quilting guild will also donate their time and sewing machines if needed.
- The batting, iron transfers, and fabric crayons will cost approximately $100, if no donors, depending on the number of participants.

Bibliography

Atkins, Jeannine. Illus. by Tad Hills. *A Name on the Quilt: A Story of Remembrance.* New York: Atheneum Books for Young Readers, 1999.
> Lauren stitches a quilt panel with her family and friends gathered together to commemorate her Uncle Ron, who died of AIDS. Their grief and remembrance of the beloved one are woven in the AIDS Memorial Quilt.

Cha, Dia. Illus. by Chue Cha and Nhia Thao Cha. *Dia's Story Cloth: The Hmong People's Journey of Freedom.* New York: Lee and Low, 1996.
> The story cloth is a quilt stitched by Dia's aunt and uncle, who fled their native Laos for a refugee camp in Thailand and ultimately came to the United States. It tells a rich story of a native Hmong family, their culture and history originating in Southeast Asia, and their American immigration story.

Hopkinson, Deborah. Illus. by James Ransome. *Sweet Clara and the Freedom Quilt.* New York: Knopf, 1993.
> Clara, a young slave girl, stitches a patchwork map that helps her make her way to freedom in Canada.

Jonas, Ann. *The Quilt.* New York: Puffin, 1994.
> A young African American girl's quilt springs to life at night.

Polacco, Patricia. *The Keeping Quilt.* New York: Simon and Schuster Books for Young Readers, 1988.
> This is the story of four generations of a Russian Jewish immigrant family, woven in a homemade quilt handed down for about a century.

Webliography

The Craft Studio. "Quilting with Children." www.thecraftstudio.com/qwc/index.htm.
> This site houses information on quilting with children. It provides a multitude of ideas and lesson plans.

The NAMES Project Foundation. "The AIDS Memorial Quilt." www.aidsquilt.org.
> This site provides directions on how you can make your own memory quilt for your loved one. The NAMES site gives you information on the current location of quilts to view.

"World Wide Quilting Page." **www.quilt.com/index.html.**

This is the oldest quilting website. It contains information for the basic quilter as well as for the advanced.

Index

The age levels, duration of program, and cost of materials in this index are approximate.
See the individual programs for more precise figures.

You may also be interested in

Risky Business: Real-world examples of risky change in action from librarians and authors of YA lit enrich this exploration of a topic rarely discussed in depth, but central to YA services in school and public libraries today.

Young Adults Deserve the Best: The first book to thoroughly expand on YALSA's Competencies in Action, *Young Adults Deserve the Best* is a key foundational tool not only for librarians but also for young adult specialists, youth advocacy professionals, and school administrators.

Quick and Popular Reads for Teens: This one-stop reference source compiles bibliographic information about the books honored by YALSA's two annual lists: *Popular Paperbacks for Young Adults* and *Quick Picks for Reluctant Readers*, which consist of recommended reading targeted at young adults who are not avid readers.

A Year of Programs for Teens 2: In this sequel to the book that "takes teen services to a new level" (Adolescence), YA experts Amy J. Alessio and Kimberly A. Patton present entirely new content with several new themed book lists and read-alikes as well as appendices with reproducible handouts for the various programs.

Order today at www.alastore.ala.org or 866-746-7252!

ALA Store purchases fund advocacy, awareness, and accreditation programs for library professionals worldwide.